THE IMPARTIAL SPECTATOR

The Impartial Spectator

Adam Smith's Moral Philosophy

D. D. RAPHAEL

CLARENDON PRESS • OXFORD

OXFORD

UNIVERSITY PRESS

Great Clarendon Street, Oxford OX2 6DP

Oxford University Press is a department of the University of Oxford.
It furthers the University's objective of excellence in research, scholarship,
and education by publishing worldwide in

Oxford New York

Auckland Cape Town Dar es Salaam Hong Kong Karachi
Kuala Lumpur Madrid Melbourne Mexico City Nairobi
New Delhi Shanghai Taipei Toronto

With offices in

Argentina Austria Brazil Chile Czech Republic France Greece
Guatemala Hungary Italy Japan Poland Portugal Singapore
South Korea Switzerland Thailand Turkey Ukraine Vietnam

Oxford is a registered trade mark of Oxford University Press
in the UK and in certain other countries

Published in the United States
by Oxford University Press Inc., New York

British Library Cataloguing in Publication Data

Data available

Library of Congress Cataloging in Publication Data

Raphael, D. D. (David Daiches), 1916–
The impartial spectator : Adam Smith's moral philosophy / D.D. Raphael.
p. cm.
Includes bibliographical references and index.
ISBN–13: 978–0–19–921333–7 (alk. paper)
ISBN–10: 0–19–921333–X (alk. paper)
1. Smith, Adam, 1723–1790. 2. Ethics, Modern—18th century.
3. Smith, Adam, 1723–1790. Theory of moral sentiments. I. Title.
B1545.Z7R37 2007
170—dc22 2006036960

Typeset by Laserwords Private Limited, Chennai, India
Printed in Great Britain
on acid-free paper by
Biddles Ltd., King's Lynn, Norfolk

ISBN 978–0–19–921333–7

1 3 5 7 9 10 8 6 4 2

Acknowledgement

Chapters 4–6 are a revised and extended version of the major part of the Dawes Hicks Lecture on Philosophy given at the British Academy in 1972, and reproduced here by kind permission from *Proceedings of the British Academy*, 58 (1972) (© The British Academy 1973).

Contents

1. Two Versions   1

2. Sympathy and Imagination   12

3. Motive and Consequences   21

4. Spectator Theory   27

5. The Impartial Spectator   32

6. Comparisons and Comment   43

7. Moral Rules   53

8. Virtue   65

9. The Cardinal Virtues   73

10. Virtue and Beauty   81

11. Ethics and Theology   94

12. Jurisprudence   105

13. Ethics and Economics   115

14. Smith's Enduring Contribution   127

Bibliography   136
Index   141

1

Two Versions

Adam Smith is known to the world as the author of *The Wealth of Nations*, a pioneering classic in the field of economics. That work was first published in 1776, when Smith was almost 53 years old. He wrote the first version of his other book, *The Theory of Moral Sentiments*, much earlier: it was published in 1759, when he was a young professor of 36. A drastically revised and expanded version, the sixth edition, appeared a few months before Smith's death in 1790 at the age of 67. The *Moral Sentiments*, unlike *The Wealth of Nations*, is not one of the great classical texts in its field, moral philosophy, but it has a prominent place among texts of the second rank. Smith himself is said to have thought it superior to *The Wealth of Nations*. Despite some long-winded sentences, the language is hardly ever obscure and the argument is easy to follow. Yet it has often been misunderstood and on that account it calls for an interpretation based on knowledge of what Smith wrote in his youth and in his relative old age.

One source of misunderstanding is that many of the commentators have been economists who have looked at the *Moral Sentiments* simply in order to find some relevance for *The Wealth of Nations*. This gave rise to the so-called Adam Smith problem, a supposed inconsistency between the psychological assumptions of the two books.

Another source of error has been a failure to note whether a particular passage was written for the first or for the sixth edition. Until the publication of the Glasgow Edition of Smith's works, most readers of the *Moral Sentiments* used a copy that reproduces the text of the sixth edition with no indication that the original version differed. And even after the Glasgow Edition became available, some otherwise well-equipped scholars, arguing a case for the views of Adam Smith, have quoted passages without looking to see whether they were written for 1759 or 1790.

An example of unfortunate failure to check whether a passage was written for 1759 or 1790 affects a paper by Professor John Dunn when he was discussing the 'practical atheism' of Smith in his later years.[1] Dunn contrasts that attitude with, as he thinks, the views of the youthful Smith who wrote in the *Moral Sentiments* that 'the very suspicion of a fatherless world, must be the most melancholy of all reflections'. That statement was in fact written by a no longer youthful Smith for the sixth edition of 1790.

A comparable error was made by Professor Jacob Viner in an important article on laissez-faire in Smith's economics.[2] He contrasted the mature realism of *The Wealth of Nations* with the youthful idealism of the *Moral Sentiments*, and quoted five passages from the ethical work as evidence for his view of it. The first of his quotations was in fact written for the far from youthful sixth edition.

A third example is a lapse in a perceptive interpretation of the *Moral Sentiments* by Professor Charles L. Griswold, bringing out the influence of drama in Smith's book.[3] He claims that, when Smith writes of the spectator's moral judgement, he envisages the spectator of a dramatic performance seeing the agent as an 'actor' on the stage. The evidence that Griswold adduces is one instance of the word

[1] John Dunn, 'From applied theology to social analysis: the break between John Locke and the Scottish Enlightenment', in Istvan Hont and Michael Ignatieff (eds.), *Wealth and Virtue* (Cambridge: Cambridge University Press, 1983), 119, 128. Dunn is in fact aware (p. 120 n.) that the sixth edition of the *Moral Sentiments* differs significantly from the earlier versions, but by an unfortunate lapse he attributes to 1759 his quotation about a fatherless world (p. 128).

[2] Jacob Viner, 'Adam Smith and Laissez Faire', *Journal of Political Economy*, 35 (1927), 198–232; repr. in Viner, *The Long View and the Short* (Glencoe, Ill., 1958).

[3] Charles L. Griswold, Jr., *Adam Smith and the Virtues of Enlightenment* (Cambridge: Cambridge University Press, 1999), 65–6, 87n. In discussing the theatrical character of the *Moral Sentiments* Griswold is much influenced by David Marshall, *The Figure of Theater* (New York: Columbia University Press, 1986). Marshall's chapter on Smith is naturally concerned only with this feature of Smith's book.

'actor' in place of 'agent' in the *Moral Sentiments* and one instance in the *Lectures on Rhetoric*. The *Moral Sentiments* instance occurs in part VI of the book, which was added to the sixth edition of 1790; so Griswold's evidence cannot apply to Smith's general conception of the spectator. There was in fact an instance of the word 'actor' in the first edition which was replaced by 'agent' in subsequent editions, showing that there was clearly no association with actors on the stage. This flaw in Griswold, however, does not lessen the value of his interpretation as a whole.

Having criticized those three scholars, I should add that several other recent commentators on Adam Smith, Professors Knud Haakonssen, Gloria Vivenza, Vivienne Brown, Stephen Darwall, Emma Rothschild, and Samuel Fleischacker, do take account of differences between the first and the sixth editions of the *Moral Sentiments*.[4] Haakonssen and Fleischacker take account also of a surviving fragment of a lecture giving a still earlier version of Smith's treatment of justice.[5] Fleischacker's book is mainly focused upon *The Wealth of Nations* but includes some subtle analysis of the *Moral Sentiments*—and indeed of the *Lectures on Jurisprudence* known to us from student reports.

An earlier commentator, Professor T. D. Campbell, was well aware of differences in the various editions of the *Moral Sentiments* and takes note of them in his book *Adam Smith's Science of Morals*.[6] Like

---

[4] Knud Haakonssen, *The Science of a Legislator* (Cambridge: Cambridge University Press, 1981), 150–1, 217; Gloria Vivenza, *Adam Smith e la cultura classica* (Pisa: Il pensiero economico moderno, 1984), 63–5; English version, revised and enlarged, *Adam Smith and the Classics* (Oxford: Oxford University Press, 2001), 54–5, 57; Vivienne Brown, *Adam Smith's Discourse* (London and New York: Routledge, 1994), 134–40; Stephen Darwall, 'Sympathetic Liberalism: Recent Work on Adam Smith', *Philosophy and Public Affairs*, 28 (1999), 153–4; Emma Rothschild, *Economic Sentiments: Adam Smith, Condorcet, and the Enlightenment* (Cambridge, Mass., and London: Harvard University Press, 2001), ch. 5; Samuel Fleischacker, *On Adam Smith's Wealth of Nations* (Princeton: Princeton University Press, 2004), 48, 83, 112–14, 148–9.

[5] See appendix II of the Glasgow Edition of Adam Smith, *The Theory of Moral Sentiments* (Oxford: Clarendon Press, 1976; corrected reprint, 1991), 389, 397. In my subsequent notes the work is cited as *TMS*.

[6] T. D. Campbell, *Adam Smith's Science of Morals* (London: George Allen & Unwin, 1971).

Fleischacker, he also considers relevant material from the lectures on jurisprudence, which he read in the actual student manuscript before it was reproduced in print. Tom Campbell is a former colleague of mine, and his book on Adam Smith is a revised version of a Ph.D. thesis that he wrote under my supervision, though I may say that he needed very little supervising, so that the book owes virtually nothing to me. I refrained from rereading it before writing this book lest it might affect what I had to say; I wanted to stick to my own thoughts, which have arisen from frequent reading of Smith's work as an editor. Having reread Campbell's book now in the final stage of preparing my own book, I have found that there is in fact very little difference between Campbell's interpretation and mine. There is, however, enough difference between the character of the two books to justify their separate existence. Campbell's book emphasizes Smith's aim to produce a work of science and discusses the moral philosophy as a part of that aim. My account goes into more detail on the particular content of the *Moral Sentiments* and suggests that the concept of the impartial spectator is especially concerned with moral judgements about one's own actions.

In contrast to my substantial agreement with Campbell, I have some criticisms to make of the views of Viner, Brown, and Fleischacker, and I shall return to them in Chapter 13. The references by Haakonssen, Vivenza, Darwall, and Rothschild to different editions of the *Moral Sentiments* do not call for comment. Vivenza's book is notable for its illuminating account of the influence of Greek and Roman thought, especially Stoicism, on Adam Smith. That is an important topic but one on which I have no particular competence and which I have therefore left alone. Haakonssen is chiefly concerned with jurisprudence. I am told that Darwall has a more substantial discussion of Smith's ethics in a book, *Second Person Standpoint*, due to be published shortly. Rothschild's discussion of Adam Smith is mainly about *The Wealth of Nations* and includes a chapter on the invisible hand, in which she is well aware of the differences between the first and sixth editions of the *Moral*

Sentiments. I am not altogether persuaded by her ingenious argument that Smith's use of the invisible hand is ironic, but it does not affect the essentials of his ethical theory.

Let me recall briefly the facts of publication of the *Moral Sentiments*. The first edition appeared in 1759. A second edition, with revisions of some substance, was published in 1761, and was followed by third, fourth, and fifth editions in the years 1767, 1774, and 1781. Revisions in those three editions were light, though not negligible in the case of the third edition. All these changes, however, including those of the second edition, are minor matters when compared with the sixth edition, which was submitted to the printer at the end of 1789 and published in May 1790. The sixth edition includes a whole new part, on the character of virtue, and some drastic revision elsewhere. My co-editor of the work, the late Professor A. L. Macfie, was apt to say in consequence that the sixth edition is a different book. That is an exaggeration, but the sixth edition is certainly a much altered book.

The primary purpose of the work is to expound a *theory* of ethics. In saying this I do not rely on the title, *The Theory of Moral Sentiments*, though that does tend to confirm what I have just said. The title is not meant to be a name for Smith's own theory: rather, it is a name for the subject matter, as we may see from the surviving manuscript fragment (mentioned above) of Smith's lecture on justice at Glasgow University. He writes there of the rules that constitute 'what is called Natural Jurisprudence, or the Theory of the general principles of Law. they make a very important part of the Theory of moral Sentiments.' That, of course, implies that Smith's own contribution is an essay in theory. However, the chief evidence of Smith's primary purpose is the content of the book: by far the largest component of it is philosophical analysis.

I stress the point because a number of commentators have laboured to derive from the book Smith's personal stance on moral questions; and at least one well-informed commentator, Professor Griswold, has emphasized Smith's 'protreptric' purpose, that is to say, his desire to promote the practice of virtue.[7] There is nothing wrong with such an approach to Smith's work. Philosophers who write on ethics do often have a particular personal stance on some moral questions, and when one of those philosophers is a famous world-figure for other reasons, it is both natural and legitimate to seek to elicit his character and personality from his writings as well as his actions. And while some philosophers, notably Smith's friend David Hume,[8] think that the philosophical explanation of ethics is muddied by mixing it with the promotion of morality, it is true enough that Smith goes in for this—though far more in the new part VI of the sixth edition than in the original work: you will find little of it if you read the first edition. The primary object of the book in all editions is to contribute to ethical theory.

When Smith wrote that natural jurisprudence is part of the theory of moral sentiments, he could just as well have said 'part of moral philosophy'. That is what he meant, taking 'moral philosophy' in the wide sense that it had for the Scottish universities of his time. Why does he call it the theory of moral *sentiments*? To answer that question one needs to recall the recent previous history of the subject.

Francis Hutcheson and David Hume were the two most prominent Scottish contributors to moral philosophy before Smith. They had criticized the view of rationalist philosophers, such as Samuel Clarke and William Wollaston, that the judgement and the motive of moral action are functions of reason, an understanding of necessary truth analogous to mathematical thinking. Hutcheson and Hume, in contrast, took the view that moral judgement is affective, rests on feeling, and that the motive for acting upon that judgement must likewise be affective, since reason alone does not have the power to stir bodily behaviour. Hume was a particularly trenchant critic: he began his discussion of morals in book III of his *Treatise of Human*

---

[7] Griswold, *Adam Smith*, ch. 1, §2, and epilogue, p. 366.

[8] Letter of 17 September 1739 to Hutcheson; *Letters of David Hume*, ed. J. Y. T. Greig (Oxford: Clarendon Press, 1932), i. 32–3. Hume is referring to the manuscript of book III of *A Treatise of Human Nature*. Some scholars think that he did not maintain this opinion in his later work.

Nature with a battery of arguments to show that 'moral distinctions' are 'not deriv'd from reason' and concluded that they are 'deriv'd from a moral sense'. He borrowed the term 'moral sense' from Hutcheson, but used it only in the title of the relevant section; in the body of his discussion he wrote instead of 'feeling' or, much more often, of 'sentiment'.

I think Adam Smith took it for granted that Hume had demonstrated beyond challenge his conclusion that moral distinctions arise from feeling. Smith therefore proceeded on the assumption that any further contribution to moral philosophy must make 'sentiment', in the sense of feeling, the basic element of its account.

The scope of Smith's contribution is relatively narrow. Its main concern is the nature of moral judgement, as is recognized in a lengthy subtitle that first appears in the fourth edition. The earlier editions had borne only the main title, 'The Theory of Moral Sentiments', but the fourth edition is more explicit: 'The Theory of Moral Sentiments, or An Essay towards an Analysis of the Principles by which Men naturally judge concerning the Conduct and Character, first of their Neighbours, and afterwards of themselves'. The analysis is of a matter of fact, the principles (general rules) that human beings do in fact follow when they pass judgement on conduct and character.

It is an explanation in terms of psychology and sociology. Adam Smith does not, like his Scottish predecessors, describe his project as an inquiry into the 'original' (Hutcheson) or 'origin' (Hume) of ethical ideas and judgements, but all three philosophers are doing the same thing, seeking a genetic explanation. Hutcheson's inquiry is conducted almost entirely in terms of psychology. Hume follows suit in the main, but brings in sociology at times—for example, when he draws an important distinction between natural and artificial virtues. With Adam Smith sociology looms larger. This is not to say that psychology recedes into the background: the psychological element in Smith's explanation of ethics is vivid, often strikingly original, and usually persuasive. It is, however, all the more illuminating for being allied with acute sociological observation.

You might say that this must limit the character of Smith's explanation of ethics: his evidence is drawn from his own society and lacks the universality that is sought by philosophers who reflect on general human experience rather than the experience of a particular section of mankind at a particular period of time. This suggestion cannot be dismissed, but it is overdrawn.

Smith certainly thought he was reflecting on general human experience, and his evidence was not limited to his own society. He had a fairly wide knowledge of history, including the history of ancient Greece and Rome, and he took a keen interest in such anthropological reports as were available, notably reports about the indigenous inhabitants of North America. He knew that the behaviour and the ethics of the American Indians differed markedly in some respects from what was found in Europe, and he knew, too, that the ethics of ancient Graeco-Roman civilization differed, in other respects, from the ethics of Christianity. He was also aware of minor differences in the mores of at least some European societies (France and Italy as compared with Britain and with each other); his description of these differences is given in the first edition of 1759, before he had set foot on the continent of Europe so as to see for himself what went on in France.

Despite all these sociological observations on variations in behaviour and moral outlook, Smith still thought he could appeal to an agreed consensus among his reflective readers on the relative merits of differing codes of conduct. He may have been too sanguine in supposing that this consensus had a universal truth. Still, even if the scope of his explanation may be limited, it remains enlightening for us today, since our ethics are not radically different from the ethics of Adam Smith's time and place.

To be sure, there have been some changes of attitude. For example, there is less deference now to 'the rich and the great' than there was in Smith's day, and a weaker trace of the ancient ethic of honour and shame that Smith finds among the 'gallant and generous part of mankind' (*TMS* I. iii. 1. 15). But such changes do not cast doubt upon Smith's explanation of moral judgement, because the sociological facts on which he relies for his explanation are of a more general nature.

He tells us that moral approval is related to the sympathetic and antipathetic feelings of spectators. If the use of those feelings changes, in respect of social status or anything else, so does the use of moral judgement: a reduction or cessation of deference to the rich and the great implies that one no longer feels a special moral obligation to meet their wishes. But the general thesis, that moral judgements depend on the feelings of spectators, remains as before. It seems impossible to imagine a set of human beings whose moral judgements are not linked to general social attitudes. Even in the fantastic fictional society of Samuel Butler's *Erewhon*, where moral condemnation is applied to illness while criminal behaviour is greeted with commiseration, both classes of judgement depend on shared social attitudes. In Hobbes's fictional state of nature, human beings are represented as influenced solely by egoistic aims; but the consequence of that, Hobbes tells us, is a complete absence of right and wrong.

Towards the beginning of the final part of the *Moral Sentiments* Smith writes:

In treating of the principles of morals there are two questions to be considered. First, wherein does virtue consist? Or what is the tone of temper, and tenour of conduct, which constitutes the excellent and praiseworthy character, the character which is the natural object of esteem, honour, and approbation? And, secondly, by what power or faculty in the mind is it, that this character, whatever it be, is recommended to us? Or in other words, how and by what means does it come to pass, that the mind prefers one tenour of conduct to another, denominates the one right and the other wrong; considers the one as the object of approbation, honour, and reward, and the other of blame, censure, and punishment? (*TMS* VII. i. 2)

One would expect such a programmatic statement to come at the beginning of the book, not near the end. It stands at the beginning of a history of moral philosophy, specifically a history of theories about the two questions that Smith says constitute the subject. There is plenty of evidence that both of Smith's books were developed from his lectures. It is also plain that his usual method of inquiry was to begin with the history of his subject and to reach his own views in the light of his survey of history. I have therefore conjectured[9] that the passage quoted above was originally the beginning of his lectures on moral philosophy and that the lectures then continued with the critical survey of history before turning to Smith's own theory.

Smith's own theory, as given in the first five editions, is for the most part a theory of moral judgement—that is to say, it is an answer to the second question set out in the initial description of the subject of philosophical ethics. I do not say that it contains nothing about the first question, the character of virtue: there is a relatively short discussion of a distinction between the 'amiable' and the 'respectable' virtues, summarized as sensibility and self-command, and a longer discussion of the contrast between justice and beneficence. But there is no thoroughgoing inquiry of what constitutes the character of virtue, as required by the first of the two questions, even though the historical survey at the end of the book deals with both questions in turn and, as it happens, gives more space to the first topic, the character of virtue, than to the second, the nature of moral judgement.

The fact is that Smith did not reach a distinctive view on the first topic. He has a distinctive view of the content of virtue, that is to say, a view of what are the cardinal virtues; but he does not give us an explanation of what is meant by the concept of moral virtue, how it arises, how it differentiates moral excellence from other forms of human excellence. The main subject matter of the first version of the book is well described in the long title added for the fourth and later editions: it is a detailed explanation of moral judgement, as passed first on the actions of other people and then on the actions of oneself. I think that, when Smith came to revise the work for the sixth edition, he realized that he had not dealt at all adequately with the first of the two questions, and for that reason he added the new part VI,

---

9 *TMS* VII. i. 2, editorial n. 1.

entitled 'Of the Character of Virtue', to remedy the omission. It is not, in my opinion, an adequate remedy, and it certainly does not match Smith's elaborate answer to the second question. It does, however, bring out the exceptional role of self-command among the virtues and thereby shows Smith's theory of virtue to be a distinct advance on that of his predecessors. Self-command has a place in the earlier version, as a marker of the 'respectable' (as contrasted with the 'amiable') virtues; in the later version it looms larger, being the determinant of a superior form of any virtue.

Since the second of the two topics, the nature of moral judgement, is the main subject of both versions of Smith's book, I shall give it priority in what follows. There is in fact a clear development in Smith's view of this topic, especially in his conception of the impartial spectator, the most important element of Smith's ethical theory. Hence the title of my book.

2

Sympathy and Imagination

The first chapter of *The Theory of Moral Sentiments* is entitled 'Of Sympathy', and the first chapter of *An Inquiry into the Nature and Causes of the Wealth of Nations* is entitled 'Of the Division of Labour'. In each instance, I think, the title is meant to indicate the primary cause of the subject matter of the book: the moral sentiments are founded on sympathy, and the increase of national wealth is founded on the division of labour. So far as the *Moral Sentiments* is concerned, the name of the primary cause has a wider sense than you might suppose. Smith notes that in common usage the term 'sympathy' tends to be limited to pity, fellow-feeling with distress, and he makes a point of telling us that he is using the term, as its etymology allows, to mean the sharing of any kind of feeling.

If, as I have suggested, the title of the first chapter is intended to pinpoint the primary cause of the book's theme, 'imagination' should be added to 'sympathy'; and of the two, imagination plays the larger part. In saying this I do not imply that sympathy is always accompanied by imagination, that sympathy, as understood by Smith, cannot get going until one has consciously imagined oneself into the shoes of another person. Smith's first examples of sympathy seem to belie that idea: they describe a spontaneous repetition of feeling and observed behaviour.

When we see a stroke aimed and just ready to fall upon the leg or arm of another person, we naturally shrink and draw back our own leg or our own arm; and when it does fall, we feel it in some measure, and are hurt by it as well as the sufferer. The mob, when they are gazing at a dancer on the slack rope, naturally writhe and twist and balance their own bodies, as they see him do, and as they feel that they themselves must do if in his situation. Persons of delicate fibres and a weak constitution of body complain, that in looking on the sores and ulcers which are exposed by beggars in the streets, they are apt to feel an itching or uneasy sensation in the correspondent part of their own bodies. (*TMS* I. i. 1. 3)

Smith himself does not distinguish such examples from explicitly imagining oneself in the place of another person. He thinks that imagination is involved in almost all instances, and he gives the examples of the above quotation to illustrate the fact that our awareness of the feelings of other people can only come from imagining ourselves in their shoes and seeing what *we* would then feel. Smith does, however, go on to mention other examples of sympathy that are entirely spontaneous and are not accompanied by the exercise of imagination.

Upon some occasions sympathy may seem to arise merely from the view of a certain emotion in another person. The passions . . . may seem to be transfused from one man to another, instantaneously . . . Grief and joy, for example, strongly expressed in the look and gestures of any one, at once affect the spectator with some degree of a like painful or agreeable emotion. A smiling face is, to every body that sees it, a cheerful object; as a sorrowful countenance, on the other hand, is a melancholy one. (*TMS* I. i. 1. 6)

Whether we think that sympathy without imagination is confined to the second set of examples or occurs in the first set also, it is a fairly unusual phenomenon. On most occasions imagination is a prerequisite for sympathy.

An explicit exercise of the imagination is certainly part of Smith's account of moral judgement. In that context imagining oneself in someone else's place is more pervasive than the actual experience of sympathy.

Let us consider first Smith's account of the judgement that an action is proper or improper. He writes also of the judgement that an affection, a feeling, is proper or improper, and here he is not confining himself to the feeling, the motive, of an agent: he would include the feeling of the person or persons affected by an action, and also the feeling of a person affected by an event, such as the death of a relative or friend. It is, however, convenient to begin with the judgement that an action is proper. In principle though not in precise detail, Smith is talking about the simple judgement that an action is right or wrong. Smith calls it a judgement of propriety or impropriety, an assertion that an action is appropriate or inappropriate, suitable or unsuitable, to the cause that has prompted the agent to do it. The primary form of such judgement, according to Smith, is made by a spectator on an action done or contemplated by another person. The spectator's judgement arises from imagining himself in the agent's place and comparing the motivating feeling of the agent with the feeling that he himself would have in the imagined situation. If his own imagined feeling is the same as the actual feeling of the agent, he is 'sympathizing' with the agent, and his awareness of the sympathy (fellow-feeling) is given expression in approval, declaring that the action is appropriate (right). If, on the other hand, his own imagined feeling differs from that of the agent, he lacks sympathy with the agent, and his awareness of this is given expression in disapproval, declaring that the action is inappropriate (wrong).[1]

Smith does not confine disapproval to a positive feeling of anti-pathy (a word that he uses very rarely), but seems to think that any degree of difference in feeling will give rise to disapproval of the action concerned. The possibilities for disapproval are therefore manifold in kind, though not necessarily more frequent than the occurrence of approval. However, the exercise of imagination is required for all the possibilities, while the experience of sympathy is

---

[1] One of the Press's advisers says some scholars claim that, 'for Smith, the very act of imaginative identification is itself an act of "sympathizing" with the agent', and he asks for textual evidence to the contrary. In his first chapter Smith defines sympathy as fellow-feeling and says that 'changing places in fancy with the sufferer' is 'the *source* of our fellow-feeling' (emphasis added). Changing places in fancy is an act of the imagination; if it is the source of fellow-feeling, it cannot be itself the fellow-feeling. The adviser gives only one name, saying that Charles Griswold, 'at moments, seems to be one such', citing Griswold's reference to Smith's example of sympathy with the dead. I think Griswold takes my view. He writes (*Adam Smith*, 90) of 'This "illusion of the imagination" *thanks to which* we sympathize with the deceased' (emphasis added): the sympathy is an effect of the act of imagination.

confined to only one of them. Hence I say that imagination is more pervasive than sympathy in the forming of moral judgements.

There are further reasons for saying that Smith thinks of imagination as more pervasive than feelings of sympathy. He notes that the moral reflection of a spectator often does not depend on any actual perception of a correspondence with, or difference from, the feeling of the agent. 'We sometimes feel for another, a passion of which he himself seems to be altogether incapable; because, when we put ourselves in his case, that passion arises in our breast from the imagination, though it does not in his from the reality' (*TMS* I. i. 1. 10). We feel compassion for the deranged (or even for the dead), because, by an 'illusion of the imagination' (*TMS* I. i. 1. 13), we attribute to them feelings of distress which they do not have but which we suppose that we, being rational instead of deranged (or being alive and conscious instead of dead), would have if we were in their situation. In these examples, as Smith portrays them, there is compassion for the deranged or the dead, but it is not a *sympathetic* compassion, because we know that the objects of our compassion are not in fact feeling distress; we are illusorily imagining a distress that we, retaining our present faculties, would feel in their situation.

Later, when he comes to deal with moral judgements on our own conduct, Smith gives the imagination an elaborate double role: we have to imagine what spectators would feel if they imagined themselves in our situation; and, while sympathy, or the lack of it, comes into the picture in characterizing the feeling of the spectators, that feeling is an *imagined* feeling; and indeed, in the end, spectators in the real world are replaced by an *imagined* impartial spectator conjured up 'in the breast'.

I come back to the starting point. A spectator observes or hears of an action done or contemplated. He knows its 'cause'; that is to say, he knows what has prompted the agent to act or think of acting. Let us suppose that the agent has come upon a child struggling to swim to the bank of a river; he dives in to help. The 'spectator' imagines himself in the agent's place and notes that he would be prompted to act likewise. In other words, he finds that he 'sympathizes' with the agent's feelings and consequent action. He gives expression to his sympathy by approving of the action as right or proper, an appropriate response to the situation.

Now suppose instead that the agent cannot himself swim. There is no point in his diving into the water; that would not help the child and would simply add a second person in danger of drowning. He cannot see a lifebelt or a rope or another passer-by, and so he takes off his shirt and uses that as a sort of rope. Let us hope that it works; anyway he thinks it is the best he can do. The 'spectator', who hears about the episode, imagines himself in the agent's shoes—and sharing the agent's inability to swim. He finds, reluctantly but inescapably, that here again he would be prompted to act in much the same way as the agent, and so he approves of the action as appropriate to the situation.

Let us now suppose that the agent meets someone who, having heard a garbled account of the incident, accuses him of cowardice. The agent, aggrieved at the taunt, punches the scoffer on the nose. When the 'spectator' learns of this and imagines himself in the agent's shoes, he finds that he too would feel aggrieved but would not be disposed to respond with a punch. Since he does not fully sympathize, he disapproves of the punch and says it was wrong, inappropriate to the situation.

The example, with its two components, illustrates the base of Smith's theory. Moral judgement begins with the reaction of spectators to the actions and motives of other people. The 'spectators' in question are normal fellow-members of society. Smith assumes that nearly all of them will react in much the same way. They include you and me, and for the most part Smith writes of what 'we' feel and think about the conduct of other people. But in key passages of his explanation he writes of 'the spectator' (occasionally 'spectators'), because the relevant feelings and thoughts that 'we' experience have come to us in our capacity as spectators. He sometimes writes of 'mankind' or 'every body', but he knows that unanimity cannot always be guaranteed and so he sometimes introduces a slight qualification, as in 'every impartial spectator' or 'every indifferent by-stander' (*TMS* ii. i. 2. 2); but, since the passage containing those phrases is almost immediately followed by 'every human heart', the qualification counts for little. Smith in fact takes it for granted that a spectator or bystander will be impartial just because he is not a party to the conduct judged.

What precisely is the relation between sympathy and approval? When introducing his theory, Smith says: 'To approve of the passions of another, therefore, as suitable to their objects, is the same thing as to observe that we entirely sympathize with them; and not to approve of them as such, is the same thing as to observe that we do not entirely sympathize with them' (*TMS* i. i. 3. 1). A little later, having compared moral approval and disapproval with approval and disapproval of opinions, Smith repeats the thesis with a slight difference of language: 'To approve or disapprove, therefore, of the opinions of others is acknowledged, by every body, to mean no more than to observe their agreement or disagreement with our own' (*TMS* i. i. 3. 2).

Approval of others 'is the same thing as', 'means no more than', observing agreement with our own attitude. Yet Smith begins the chapter by saying this:

When the original passions of the person principally concerned are in perfect concord with the sympathetic emotions of the spectator, they necessarily appear to this last just and proper, and suitable to their objects; and, on the contrary, when, upon bringing the case home to himself, he finds that they do not coincide with what he feels, they necessarily appear to him unjust and improper, and unsuitable to the causes which excite them. (*TMS* i. i. 3. 1)

That passage surely gives a different *meaning* to the two clauses of each statement; it makes the spectator's judgement an effect, a necessary consequence, of his finding a correspondence, or a lack of correspondence, in feeling. Likewise, after saying that approval 'is the same thing' as awareness of sympathy, Smith continues with further statements implying a relation of cause and effect, not of identity proper, a relation of factual, not logical, necessity.

The man who resents the injuries that have been done to me, and observes that I resent them precisely as he does, necessarily approves of my resentment. The man whose sympathy keeps time to my grief, cannot but admit the reasonableness of my sorrow. He who admires the same poem, or the same picture, and admires them exactly as I do, must surely allow the justness of my admiration. He who laughs at the same joke, and laughs along with me, cannot well deny the propriety of my laughter. (*TMS* i. i. 3. 1)

The spectator 'must surely allow', 'cannot well deny', propriety. These expressions would be out of place if approval were 'the same thing', had 'the same meaning', as awareness of sympathy.

More decisively still, when Smith proceeds to give examples of the apparent incidence of approval 'without any sympathy or correspondence of sentiments', he says: 'A little attention, however, will convince us that even in these cases our approbation is ultimately founded upon a sympathy or correspondence of this kind' (*TMS* i. i. 3. 3). Approval that is 'founded upon' sympathy is undoubtedly an effect and cannot be simply identified with awareness of the sympathy.

The identity view is in any event far-fetched, while the causal connection view seems a reasonable account of the psychological explanation that Smith has in mind. I conclude that the two statements of identity are a rhetorical lapse, intended to emphasize the necessity of the connection between sympathy and approval.

Smith clarifies his position in a footnote added to the second edition (*TMS* i. iii. 1. 9). The purpose of the footnote is to answer a criticism of Hume querying an apparent implication that all sympathy is pleasant, a view inconsistent with the plain fact that sympathy can be a sharing of painful feelings: Smith himself, Hume writes, rightly says that 'it is painful to go along with grief'. Smith takes the objection to be concerned with his theory of approval: 'It has been objected to me that as I found the sentiment of approbation, which is always agreeable, upon sympathy, it is inconsistent with my system to admit any disagreeable sympathy.' Smith replies by describing two different feelings involved in the sentiment of approbation: first, the spectator's feeling of sympathy with the feeling of the person judged, which can be either pleasant or unpleasant; secondly, 'the emotion which arises' from the spectator's awareness of the correspondence between the feelings of the two persons. 'This last emotion, in which the sentiment of approbation properly consists, is always agreeable and delightful.' So here Smith distinguishes between the feeling of sympathy, the observation of correspondence, and a consequent emotion which is the feeling of approbation. This is a more elaborate analysis than that given in the ambiguous statements of the first edition.

In one of the quotations given above, Smith compares moral with aesthetic judgement: he says that the man who sympathizes with my resentment or my grief must approve of my feelings as appropriate, and he then goes on to compare this with sharing, and consequently approving of, my admiration of a poem or a picture, or my enjoyment of a joke. This is not to say that the morally approved feelings, resentment (of injury) or grief (in bereavement, for example), are similar in character to the aesthetic feelings of admiring the beautiful or enjoying the comic. It is to say that the spectator's *approval* is similar in the two types of experience. Elsewhere, as we shall see in due course, Smith has more detailed views about an affinity between ethics and aesthetics. Here he is simply emphasizing the connection between sympathy and approval by noting that it is not confined to moral approval. He finds such a connection in a concord of aesthetic reaction too, and even in a concord of opinion. After elaborating the effect of concordance or discordance in the moral and aesthetic examples, Smith turns to opinion.

To approve of another man's opinions is to adopt those opinions, and to adopt them is to approve of them. If the same arguments which convince you convince me likewise, I necessarily approve of your conviction; and if they do not, I necessarily disapprove of it; neither can I possibly conceive that I should do the one without the other. To approve or disapprove, therefore, of the opinions of others is acknowledged, by every body, to mean no more than to observe their agreement or disagreement with our own. (*TMS* I. i. 3. 2)

Here again we find Smith saying that the expression of approval *means* the same as being aware of a concord. As before, he is led into error by his emphasis on concordance. He reasonably says, in the second sentence, that he approves of another man's opinion if that opinion has been reached by attention to argument which he himself has found convincing. So the ground for approval of the other person's opinion, as for his own acceptance of the opinion, is that there is (what he takes to be) sound argument for the opinion, not the mere fact that he himself shares the opinion.

At the end of the chapter Smith lets himself be carried away into a ridiculous generalization of the concordance view.

Every faculty in one man is the measure by which he judges of the like faculty in another. I judge of your sight by my sight, of your ear by my ear, of your reason by my reason, of your resentment by my resentment, of your love by my love. I neither have, nor can have, any other way of judging about them. (*TMS* I. i. 3. 10)

This is certainly not true of 'every faculty'. I am short-sighted and would not dream of judging the accuracy of another man's sight by my own. In my old age I am a little deaf and would therefore not trust my ear as a criterion of the ear of others. Knowing that some people have perfect pitch, I would never have been so foolhardy as to judge their capacity to distinguish tones by my own capacity to do so. Smith is simply wrong in saying that we have no other way of judging all the faculties of other people. In the case of sight and hearing we can judge by other forms of perception. When my neighbour sees a firm straight edge where I see a fuzzy one, I can check by touch. If he hears a sound when I do not, I can check by consulting a third person, known to have acute hearing. Smith's aim in this discussion is to persuade us of the relevance of sympathy to moral approval and disapproval. It is necessary and reasonable to show how this applies to resentment. It is quite unnecessary, and indeed counter-productive, to bring in the judgement of opinion, and then of 'every faculty'.

3

Motive and Consequences

In portraying the role of sympathy in moral judgement, is Smith right to confine himself to sympathy with motive? My criticism of his comparison between moral approval and other forms of approval (of opinion and of sense perception) notes that the latter kinds of approval do not depend on concord of experience but on a different, an objective, fact: the opinion is approved because it is supported by sound argument; the faculty of sight or hearing is credited because its deliverances are supported by those of another sense or because it shows acute discrimination. Is not the same sort of thing true of moral approval? When you approve of another person's action, declaring it to be right or proper, is not your approval based on some feature of the action rather than the mere thought that you would be moved to do the same thing? After all, one can ask why *you* would be moved to do the same thing, and the answer must lie in a feature of the action, such as good consequences or being the fulfilment of a promise. And your approval, as spectator, of the like action of another person depends similarly on that feature of the action, as does Smith's approval of an opinion that has been reached (either by himself or by another person) as the result of sound argument.

The relevant features of an action include its effects on some other person or persons, and here imaginative sympathy has an important role. In judging whether the action is right or wrong, you must take account of what it does to other people: does it help or hurt, meet a need, fulfil an expectation? You form an idea of such effects on other people by imagining yourself in their place and assuming that they feel what you would feel. Why does Smith not write of this exercise of sympathy?

He does, but in his account of merit, not in his account of propriety. He tells us, in his chapter on the judgement of propriety, that recent philosophers, when discussing the judgement of conduct, have mainly considered intended or probable effects and have neglected motive, while judgement in common life takes account of both. He is thinking chiefly of Hume, though perhaps also of Hutcheson. He then goes on to say, quite rightly, that, when we blame in others an excess of love, grief, or resentment, we are thinking not only of bad effects but also of the little ground given for an extravagant reaction. So one would expect Smith to avoid the one-sided approach of recent philosophers and to include both motive and intended effects in his own analysis. Curiously, however, he has decided that the two elements belong to different forms of moral judgement: a judgement of propriety or impropriety depends on thought about motive, while a judgement of merit or demerit depends on thought about intended effects.

The sentiment or affection of the heart from which any action proceeds, and upon which its whole virtue or vice must ultimately depend, may be considered under two different aspects, or in two different relations; first, in relation to the cause which excites it, or the motive which gives occasion to it; and secondly, in relation to the end which it proposes, or the effect which it tends to produce.

In the suitableness or unsuitableness, in the proportion or disproportion which the affection seems to bear to the cause or object which excites it, consists the propriety or impropriety, the decency or ungracefulness of the consequent action.

In the beneficial or hurtful nature of the effects which the affection aims at, or tends to produce, consists the merit or demerit of the action, the qualities by which it is entitled to reward, or is deserving of punishment. (*TMS* I. i. 3. 5–7)

The first sentence of this quotation seems to imply that, for Smith, *all* moral judgements are judgements about the 'sentiment or affection' of the agent, about motive and intention, about 'virtue and vice'; and this would exclude judgements about the character of the actions performed. If so, it is incorrect to say, as I have said, that 'propriety' and 'impropriety' are, in principle, expressions for right and wrong. But note that Smith goes on to treat intended effects as equivalent to probable effects, the effects that a particular feeling 'tends to produce'. Since this expression, given in the initial paragraph of the quotation, is then repeated in the third paragraph, about merit, we must take it to be Smith's considered view, and consequently we must infer that the first words of the quotation are less considered and in fact inaccurate. Smith does not think that moral judgements upon actions are always and only concerned with the state of mind of the agent. He holds that the merit or demerit of an action is constituted by its intended *or probable* consequences.

His words on this score could be taken to mean that intended consequences ('the end which [the affection] proposes', 'the effects which the affection aims at') are the same as probable consequences ('the effect which it tends to produce'); but Smith could hardly have been so slipshod as that. It is more likely that the two notions, intended consequences and probable consequences, are alternative possibilities. In legal practice, a person is presumed to intend the probable consequences of his or her actions, and Smith was no doubt familiar with that. The presumption is not taken to be always true; it is taken to be generally true, reliable enough to be followed when direct knowledge of intention is not available. So we may suppose Smith's view to be that a judgement of merit is ideally based on intention and may in practice be based on probable consequences as evidence of intention.

What about the judgement of propriety? Smith says that this consists in the 'suitableness or ... proportion' that the motivating affection bears to 'the cause or object which excites it' or 'the motive which gives occasion to it'. This is rather obscure. One would suppose that 'the cause or object which excites it' might be some experience of the person whose action is commended or blamed as proper or improper. Or it might be some action of another person that has affected the person of whom we speak. But then Smith gives the alternative of 'the motive which gives occasion to it'. Does he mean the motive of an action of another person, an action that has given rise to the action now praised or blamed? Or does he mean the motive of the latter action itself? The second possibility would require us to understand 'it' ('the motive which gives occasion to it') as meaning the action; but, from what has gone before, 'it' should be the agent's 'affection', which of course is the motive of his action.

Illustrating the point in the paragraph that follows the above quotation, Smith refers to excesses of feeling that we blame as disproportionate.

Philosophers have, of late years, considered chiefly the tendency of affections, and have given little attention to the relation which they stand in to the cause which excites them. In common life, however, when we judge of any person's conduct, and of the sentiments which directed it, we constantly consider them under both these aspects. When we blame in another man the excesses of love, of grief, of resentment, we not only consider the ruinous effects which they tend to produce, but the little occasion which was given for them. The merit of his favourite, we say, is not so great, his misfortune is not so dreadful, his provocation is not so extraordinary, as to justify so violent a passion. (*TMS* I. i. 3. 8)

Here the judgement of blame is directed both upon 'conduct' and upon 'the sentiments which directed it'. Smith goes on to specify certain sentiments, so these must have been in the forefront of his thoughts; but he continues to include the 'effects which they tend to produce'. It is still unclear whether both elements are present in a judgement of propriety.

However, the two short paragraphs referring explicitly, first to propriety, and then to merit, seem to show clearly enough that Smith analyses the first as a judgement of the motive of action, and the second as a judgement of intended or probable consequences. They seem to imply that the analysis is complete, so that a judgement of propriety is *only* about motive and does not also include thought about consequences.

If so, Smith is undoubtedly mistaken. I may be mistaken in identifying Smith's propriety and impropriety with right and wrong: he thinks more of judging agents than of judging actions. Even so, moral judgements on agents include thought about consequences. Smith recognizes that they are concerned with intentions as well as motives. A person's intention in doing an action goes well beyond the purely physical movement initiated: it has an aim, to bring about some effect or effects of the physical movement. Smith complains, fairly enough, that an analysis of moral judgement is too narrow if it refers simply to intended (or probable) consequences. He tries to make his point forcefully by stressing the distinction between intended consequences and motive. He thus gets carried away into concluding that the two things have quite distinct roles in moral judgement, that, in fact, they belong to two different forms of such judgement.

We have to conclude that Smith's portrayal of the role of sympathy in judgements of propriety is unduly limited. He represents it as sympathy with motive alone, instead of including also sympathy with intended or probable consequences.

It is possible that he was led into this error because he was keen to distinguish his theory from Hume's. His theory was indeed different, and in some respects an advance on Hume—but not in this particular matter of the role of sympathy. Hume introduced the concept of sympathy, sharing the feelings of those *affected* by an action, to explain approval and disapproval of the action. It offered a psychological explanation of approval and disapproval where Hutcheson had simply given a name, 'moral sense', to the capacity for approval and disapproval. The result was to focus attention on the consequences of the action judged. Smith saw that this was too narrow a view, but, instead of accepting its partial truth and simply adding to it, he was (I surmise) misled into replacing it, in judgements of right and wrong, by a different form of sympathy, and dispatching Hume's concept of sympathy to judgements of merit.

He may well have been influenced by the fact that Hume used the term 'merit' for moral appraisal in general when he wrote his second account of ethics in *An Enquiry into the Principles of Morals*. The history of the concept of sympathy in Hume and Smith is worth some special attention.

4

Spectator Theory

A theory of moral judgement based upon the feelings of spectators is found in three Scottish philosophers, Hutcheson, Hume, and Adam Smith, all three being empiricists. In the history of British moral philosophy, rationalist theories of moral judgement begin from the standpoint of the moral agent. So do those empiricist theories that presuppose an egoistic psychology.

Francis Hutcheson was not the first empiricist philosopher to question an egoistic psychology, but he probably was the first to insist that there are disinterested judgements about the moral character of actions as well as disinterested motives for doing or refraining from those actions. Lord Shaftesbury and Bishop Butler both argued for disinterested motives, but neither of them could fully shake off the conviction that a judgement to justify doing or refraining from an action must in the last resort be based on self-interest. Shaftesbury thought it necessary to ask 'what obligation there is to virtue; or what reason to embrace it', and to answer the question by showing 'that moral rectitude, or virtue, must accordingly be the advantage, and vice the injury and disadvantage of every creature'.[1] Butler likewise thought it necessary to 'allow' that 'when we sit down in a cool hour, we can neither justify to ourselves this [virtue or moral rectitude]

---

[1] Anthony Ashley Cooper, 3rd Earl of Shaftesbury, *An Inquiry concerning Virtue, or Merit* (corrected 2nd edn., 1714), II. i. 1; D. D. Raphael (ed.), *British Moralists 1650–1800* (Oxford: Clarendon Press, 1969; repr. Indianapolis: Hackett, 1991), §§205, 207.

or any other pursuit, till we are convinced that it will be for our happiness, or at least not contrary to it'.[2]

At any rate, whether or not influenced by this conviction, Shaftesbury and Butler gave accounts of moral judgement in terms of the psychology of the moral agent alone. They spoke of the agent reflecting upon his motives and thereby forming a judgement. Hutcheson struck out a new path in saying that a judgement of approving another person's action could be quite disinterested, uninfluenced by any thought of benefit to oneself. He attributed the feeling of approval to the moral sense. Shaftesbury had used the expression 'moral sense', but only casually, as it is (and was in his time) used in ordinary speech; he did not adopt it to express the moral sense theory proper. That was invented by Hutcheson.

The moral sense, as understood by Hutcheson, is a disinterested feeling of approval naturally evoked when we come across the disinterested motive of benevolence, and a similar feeling of disapproval for motives with a tendency opposed to that of benevolence. Hutcheson compared the moral sense with the disinterested feeling of love or admiration aroused by objects that we call beautiful. In making that comparison Hutcheson was not saying quite that virtue and beauty are wholly in the heart of the beholder; for the objects of moral approval and aesthetic admiration respectively have their own particular character: in Hutcheson's view, moral approval is directed upon benevolence, and aesthetic admiration is directed upon unity-in-variety. Nevertheless benevolence alone does not constitute virtue for Hutcheson, and unity-in-variety alone does not constitute beauty. Virtue is benevolence approved, and beauty is unity-in-variety admired. The reaction of a spectator is a necessary though not a sufficient condition.

Since Hutcheson was at pains to stress the disinterestedness of moral approval and disapproval, he had to concentrate on the

---

[2] Joseph Butler, Sermon XI (in *Fifteen Sermons preached at the Rolls Chapel* (1726)); Raphael (ed.), *British Moralists*, §423.

reaction of a spectator; approval of benevolence by the agent himself may well be, and approval by the beneficiary is almost bound to be, an interested approval. It is not surprising, then, that Hutcheson should often refer to 'spectators' or 'observers' in explaining his views. (I have added the italics in the quotations as given here.)

'Virtue is then called amiable or lovely, from its raising good-will or love in *spectators* toward the agent.'[3] 'Does not *every spectator* approve the pursuit of public good more than private?'[4] 'It is more probable, when our actions are really kind and publicly useful, that *all observers* shall . . . approve what we approve ourselves.'[5] 'Do these words [merit, praise-worthiness] denote the quality in actions, which gains approbation from *the observer* . . . Or, 2dly, are these actions called meritorious, which, when *any observer* does approve, *all other observers* approve him for his approbation . . .'[6]

Hume added to this theory an explanation of the moral sense or 'moral sentiment', the capacity to feel approval or disapproval. These feelings, he said, are feelings of pleasure or displeasure of a particular kind, and they arise from *sympathy* with the pleasure or pain of the person or persons affected by the action judged. Benevolence pleases the observer because he sympathizes with the pleasure that benevolent action brings to the benefited; ill will displeases the observer because he sympathizes with the displeasure that malevolent action brings to the person(s) affected.

Hume did not follow Hutcheson in confining virtue to benevolence. That was too simple a scheme, and Hume saw that a satisfactory theory needed to give a more complex account of the virtues. Some of them were 'natural' virtues, praiseworthy tendencies

[3] Francis Hutcheson, *An Inquiry concerning Moral Good and Evil*, in *An Inquiry into the original of our Ideas of Beauty and Virtue* (rev. 4th edn., 1738), I. viii; Raphael (ed.), *British Moralists*, §314.

[4] Francis Hutcheson, *Illustrations upon the Moral Sense*, in *An Essay on the Nature and Conduct of the Passions and Affections. With Illustrations on the Moral Sense* (1728; 3rd edn., 1742), I; Raphael (ed.), *British Moralists*, §362.

[5] Hutcheson, *Illustrations*, IV; Raphael (ed.), *British Moralists*, §370.

[6] Hutcheson, *Illustrations*, V; Raphael (ed.), *British Moralists*, §373.

that arose simply, spontaneously, benevolence being the most prominent, though not the sole, example. Other virtues required a context
of social practice as well as a natural tendency; Hume called these
'artificial' virtues, the most prominent example being justice. Notwithstanding these complexities, however, Hume founded all moral
approval essentially on sympathy. Like Hutcheson, he analysed moral
judgement from the point of view of a spectator. 'The hypothesis
which we embrace . . . defines virtue to be *whatever mental action or
quality gives to a spectator the pleasing sentiment of approbation*; and
vice the contrary.'[7]

Hume distinguished the language of morals from the language of
self-love. The language of morals, in being disinterested, expresses
feelings common to all mankind. When a man speaks the language of self-love, he expresses sentiments 'arising from his particular
circumstances and situation'; but when he speaks the language of
morals, he must 'depart from his private and particular situation,
and must choose a point of view, common to him with others: He
must move some universal principle of the human frame, and touch
a string, to which all mankind have an accord and symphony'.[8]
The 'sentiments' that Hume's spectator expresses are impartial and
(in a sense) rational: impartial because disinterested, and rational
because universal. In one place Hume wrote of 'a judicious spectator',[9] and elsewhere of 'every spectator'.[10] The concept, though
not the precise name, of an impartial spectator is there already in
Hume.

---

[7] David Hume, *An Enquiry concerning the Principles of Morals*, app. 1, para. 10; in
Enquiries concerning the Human Understanding and concerning the Principles of Morals,
ed. L. A. Selby-Bigge (Oxford: Clarendon Press, 1893; rev. P. H. Nidditch, 1975), §239;
ed. Tom L. Beauchamp (Oxford: Clarendon Press, 1998), 85–6.

[8] *Enquiry*, 9. i, para. 6; ed. Selby-Bigge, §222; ed. Beauchamp, 75.

[9] David Hume, *A Treatise of Human Nature*, III. iii. 1, para. 14; ed. L. A. Selby-Bigge
(Oxford: Clarendon Press, 1896; rev. P. H. Nidditch, 1978), 581; ed. David Fate Norton
and Mary J. Norton (Oxford: Oxford University Press, 2000), 371. Hutcheson, too,
used this expression in his lectures, published posthumously in 1755 as *A System of Moral
Philosophy*, i. 235.

[10] *Treatise*, III. iii. 1, para. 30; ed. Selby-Bigge, 591; ed. Norton, 377; *Enquiry*, v. i,
para. 1; ed. Selby-Bigge, §172; ed. Beauchamp, 33.

What is original in Adam Smith is the development of the concept so as to explain the judgements of conscience made by an agent about his own actions. A spectator theory accounts most easily for judgements made in the third person (judgements about 'him', 'her', or 'them') and well enough for second-person judgements (those about 'you'); but it is apt to be in difficulties with judgements made in the first person (about 'me' or 'us'). A spectator theory is also more comfortable with passing verdicts on what has been done in the past than with considering and deciding what should be done in the future.

Ethical rationalists concentrated on the idea of duty and on a criterion for determining one's duty. Hutcheson and Hume thought more of virtue and the assessment of virtue by third parties; on the idea of duty or obligation they were decidedly weak. Adam Smith followed the path of Hutcheson and Hume in his initial thought, giving an account of moral judgement in terms of the feelings of spectators when they reflect on a person's action, being themselves unaffected by it. That, however, was just the initial thought. As one might expect, Smith wanted to make an independent contribution to the line of thought pursued by his teacher Hutcheson and his friend Hume.

Hume had clearly improved upon Hutcheson's simple moral sense theory by giving a psychological explanation of moral approval in terms of sympathy. The sympathy to which Hume referred was a spectator's sympathy with the feelings of the person or persons affected by the action concerned. Smith thought he could do better by adding to the explanation a reference to the spectator's sympathy with the feelings, the motive, of the agent. He did also retain Hume's reference to sympathy with the feelings of those affected by the action, but he brought this into his account of merit and demerit, not into his account of right and wrong ('propriety' and 'impropriety'). I have tried to show in Chapter 3 that this was a lapse on his part: his account of a judgement of right and wrong is less satisfactory than Hume's. But Smith did go on to consider the judgement of an agent on his own action, and here he made a signal advance on the thought of Hume—and, of course, on the thought of Hutcheson too.

5

The Impartial Spectator

Adam Smith's theory of the impartial spectator did not, like Athena, spring fully armed at its first appearance from the head of its creator. A distinct development can be seen in changes made, both in the second edition of the *Moral Sentiments*, published a couple of years after the first, and in the sixth edition, published thirty years later. The changes in the sixth edition are major, and I shall discuss their relevance in due course. A letter from Smith to Sir Gilbert Elliot, dated 10 October 1759 (a few months after the publication of the first edition), shows that a substantial addition in the second edition, elaborating Smith's view of the impartial spectator, was composed in response to a criticism made privately to Smith by Elliot.

I believe there is evidence enough to say that the earliest version of Smith's lectures on moral philosophy did not contain the theory of the impartial spectator at all. Glasgow University Library possesses a short manuscript that is unquestionably, in my opinion, the latter part of one of Smith's lectures on ethics, the original source of *The Theory of Moral Sentiments*.[1] (As I have noted in Chapter 1, the manuscript contains that expression as his name for the subject of moral philosophy.) In this fragment there is no mention of the impartial spectator, although much of the discussion is concerned with reactions that go to form the sense of justice and the measure of just punishment. Smith spoke of what 'we' feel, of 'our heart' or of

---

[1] I have published the text, and have discussed several questions affecting the manuscript, in an article entitled 'Adam Smith and "the infection of David Hume's society"', *Journal of the History of Ideas*, 30 (1969), 225–48. The article, with a minor correction, is reprinted as appendix II of the Glasgow Edition of the *Moral Sentiments*.

'mankind' naturally applauding a punishment. In one place he wrote that the magistrate who hears a complaint of injustice 'promises . . . to give that redress which to any impartial person shall appear to be just and equitable'; and when he reproduced this passage in the *Moral Sentiments* it became simply 'the magistrate . . . promises to hear and to redress every complaint of injury' (*TMS* vii. iv. 36).[2] The word 'impartial', occurring as it does in the manuscript, is significant only of its normal usage in the context of justice and equity. Since Smith wrote 'any impartial *person*', he clearly had not, at this date (*c.* 1752), formulated the doctrine of the impartial spectator.

Nor had he done so when he first wrote the shorter form of words that eventually appeared in the *Moral Sentiments*. In the lecture Smith said that there was no precise rule for determining the proper degree of resentment or punishment, and that this aspect of justice (though not others) was loose and indeterminate, like beneficence. By 1759, when the *Moral Sentiments* was first printed, he had reached the view that there *was* a precise criterion: the proper degree of resentment or punishment was the degree that aroused 'the sympathetic indignation of the spectator' (*TMS* ii. ii. 2. 1–2).

In editing *The Theory of Moral Sentiments* I spent many days collating the text of all editions published in Adam Smith's lifetime and working out the exact nature of the revisions he introduced. That kind of exercise gives one an eye for spotting earlier and later composition. There are many passages in the *Moral Sentiments* which appear to me to come from an early draft and which, like the manuscript lecture on justice, speak of moral judgements as expressing the feelings, not of a 'spectator', but of 'us' or 'mankind' or 'other people' or 'the company' or 'strangers'; 'we' and 'mankind' are especially common. Smith's theory, no less than the theories of Hutcheson and Hume, begins from the spectator's point of view, but it does not need to stress the word 'spectator' at that stage. Nor does it need Adam Smith's special concept of the *impartial* spectator

---

[2] This reference is to the 6th and subsequent edns., but the words were written for the 1st edn. and remained unchanged.

so long as it is confined to judgements made in the second or the third person. The spectator is 'indifferent' in the sense of not being an interested party, and he expresses a universal point of view in being representative of any observer with normal human feelings. For Adam Smith, however, the theory of Hutcheson and Hume could be stated in terms of 'mankind' or 'strangers' quite as well as in terms of 'spectators'.

Smith began to stress the impartiality of the spectator only when he came to theorize about the *effect on the agent* of the reactions of spectators. Smith's spectator is first called 'impartial' in the chapter that distinguishes between 'the amiable and the respectable virtues', the virtues of humanity, on the one hand, and self-command, on the other. Humanity is a more-than-average degree of sympathetic feeling and is the result of an effort by the spectator to heighten his sympathy so as to match the experience of 'the person principally concerned'. Self-command is conversely a virtue of 'the person principally concerned' and is the result of an endeavour to restrain natural emotion and to lower its pitch to that which the ordinary (not the especially humane) spectator feels by sympathy. It is in this latter context that Smith first used the phrase 'the impartial spectator' (*TMS* I. i. 5. 4).

Humanity and self-command together constitute for Smith 'the perfection of human nature', a combination of Christian and Stoic virtue. 'As to love our neighbour as we love ourselves is the great law of Christianity, so it is the great precept of nature to love ourselves only as we love our neighbour, or what comes to the same thing, as our neighbour is capable of loving us' (*TMS* I. i. 5. 5). Self-command is essentially to feel for ourselves only what we see others can feel for us.[3]

So too, according to Adam Smith, the approval and disapproval of oneself that we call conscience is an effect of judgements made

---

[3] In III. 4. 6 Smith writes of seeing ourselves 'in the light in which others see us, or in which they would see us if they knew all'. Professor A. L. Macfie (*The Individual in Society: Papers on Adam Smith* (London: Allen & Unwin, 1967), 66) remarked that this must surely have inspired Robert Burns's 'To see oursels as others see us', since Burns knew and valued Smith's book.

by spectators. Each of us judges others as a spectator. Each of us finds spectators judging him. We then come to judge our own conduct by imagining whether an impartial spectator would approve or disapprove of it. 'We examine it as we imagine an impartial spectator would examine it' (*TMS.* III. 1. 2).[4] Conscience is a social product, a mirror of social feeling. Without society, Smith wrote, a man 'could no more think of his own character ... of the beauty or deformity of his own mind, than of the beauty or deformity of his own face'. For both he needs a mirror. The mirror in which he can view his character 'is placed in the countenance and behaviour of those he lives with' (*TMS* III. 1. 3). We are all anxious to stand well with our fellows.

We begin, upon this account, to examine our own passions and conduct, and to consider how these must appear to them. ... We suppose ourselves the spectators of our own behaviour, and endeavour to imagine what effect it would, in this light, produce upon us. This is the only looking-glass by which we can, in some measure, with the eyes of other people, scrutinize the propriety of our own conduct. (*TMS* III. 1. 5)

The 'supposed impartial spectator', as Smith often called him, is not the actual bystander who may express approval or disapproval of my conduct. He is a creation of my imagination. He is indeed myself, though in the character of an imagined spectator, not in the character of an agent.

To judge of ourselves as we judge of others ... is the greatest exertion of candour and impartiality. In order to do this, we must look at ourselves with the same eyes with which we look at others: we must imagine ourselves not the actors, but the spectators of our own character and conduct. ... We must enter, in short, either into what are, or into what ought to be, or into what, if the whole circumstances of our conduct were known, we imagine would be the sentiments of others, before we can either applaud or condemn it.[5]

---

[4] This is the wording of the 1st–5th edns. The 6th edn. expands the sentence to: 'We endeavour to examine our own conduct as we imagine any other fair and impartial spectator would examine it.'

[5] This passage appeared in the 1st edn. following what is now III. 1. 3.

On revising this passage for the second edition Smith was more explicit:

> When I endeavour to examine my own conduct . . . it is evident that . . . I divide myself, as it were, into two persons; and that I, the examiner and judge, represent a different character from that other I, the person whose conduct is examined into and judged of. The first is the spectator. . . . The second is the agent . . . (*TMS* III. 1. 6)

The impartial spectator, 'the man within', may judge differently from the actual spectator, 'the man without'. The voice of conscience reflects what I imagine that I, with all my knowledge of the situation, would feel if I were a spectator instead of an agent.

It is easy to miss this distinction and to suppose that conscience for Smith is purely a reflection of actual social attitudes. The misunderstanding is especially easy if one concentrates on a passage that, in the first edition, appeared at an early stage in the discussion:

> To be amiable and to be meritorious; that is, to deserve love and to deserve reward, are the great characters of virtue; and to be odious and punishable, of vice. But all these characters have an immediate reference to the sentiments of others. Virtue is not said to be amiable, or to be meritorious, because it is the object of its own love, or of its own gratitude; but because it excites those sentiments in other men. The consciousness that it is the object of such favourable regards, is the source of that inward tranquillity and self-satisfaction with which it is naturally attended, as the suspicion of the contrary gives occasion to the torments of vice. (*TMS* III. 1. 7)

The view that conscience reflects actual social attitudes faces a difficulty: if this view were correct, how could conscience ever go against popular opinion, as it clearly sometimes does? This must have been the objection put to Smith by Sir Gilbert Elliot in a letter written soon after the publication of the first edition of the *Moral Sentiments*. Smith replied on 10 October 1759 and sent Elliot a copy of a lengthy revision obviously written as an instruction to the printer.[6] In his letter he wrote of his intention in making the revision: 'You will observe that it is intended both to confirm my Doctrine that our judgements concerning our own conduct have always a reference to the sentiments of some other being, and to shew that, notwithstanding this, real magnanimity and conscious virtue can support itselfe under the disapprobation of all mankind.'

The revision that accompanied Smith's letter differs in some slight details from the version that was subsequently incorporated in the second edition of the book, published late in 1760 (and imprinted 1761). In principle, however, the development of the doctrine of the impartial spectator in the second edition was due to the objection made by Elliot.

On the one hand, Smith wanted to retain the traditional view that the voice of conscience represents the voice of God and is superior to popular opinion. On the other hand, he believed that conscience is initially an effect of social approval and disapproval; in the first instance, *vox populi* is *vox Dei*. 'The author of nature has made man the immediate judge of mankind, and has, in this respect, as in many others, created him after his own image, and appointed him his vicegerent upon earth to superintend the behaviour of his brethren.'[7] Although the developed conscience is a superior tribunal, 'yet, if we enquire into the origin of its institution, its jurisdiction, we shall find, is in a great measure derived from the authority of that very tribunal, whose decisions it so often and so justly reverses'.[8]

How, then, does the superior tribunal acquire its independence? We find by experience that our first fond hopes of winning everyone's approval are unattainable: 'by pleasing one man, we ... disoblige another.' In practice bystanders tend to be biased by partiality and ignorance. And so we imagine an impartial spectator.

[6] The letter and the accompanying revision are printed as Letter 40 in *The Correspondence of Adam Smith*, ed. E. C. Mossner and I. S. Ross (Oxford: Clarendon Press, 1977; 2nd edn., 1987).

[7] *TMS* iii. 2. 31, but as it appears in the draft sent to Elliot and in the 2nd edn.

[8] This quotation, and the two that follow it, occur shortly after the preceding one in the draft sent to Elliot and in the 2nd edn., but were removed from the 6th edn. See paragraph about Jean Calas below.

We conceive ourselves as acting in the presence of a person quite candid and equitable, of one who has no particular relation either to ourselves, or to those whose interests are affected by our conduct, who is neither father, nor brother, nor friend either to them or to us, but is merely a man in general, an impartial spectator who considers our conduct with the same indifference with which we regard that of other people.

Smith then went on to describe the impartial spectator as 'this inmate of the breast, this abstract man, the representative of mankind, and substitute of the Deity'. As in perception, true judgements require the use of imagination. Smith illustrated the analogy with the example of his perceiving distant hills through the windows of his study. To the eye the hills are enclosed within the small space of the window frame; in order to obtain a true judgement of the relative sizes of the vista and the window, one needs to imagine oneself at roughly equal distances from both.[9]

It is significant that at one place the second edition dropped a paragraph that had appeared in the first about the unreliability of the imagination as a 'moral looking-glass'. In the first edition, after writing of the function of the imagination as the mirror in which we see our own character, Smith had added that, while ordinary mirrors can conceal deformities, 'there is not in the world such a smoother of wrinkles as is every man's imagination, with regard to the blemishes of his own character'.[10] Excluding the paragraph in the second edition, Smith trusted the imagination more and society less.

This process was carried further in the sixth edition, where Smith wrote that it was the mark of vanity to be flattered by the praise of society and to ignore the truer judgement of conscience. Evidently he still felt the force of Sir Gilbert Elliot's objection that conscience was independent of social attitudes.

Experience of the world had in fact made him more distrustful of popular opinion. He was especially moved by the fate of Jean

---

[9] In the 6th edn. this comparison appears at III. 3. 2.
[10] The paragraph followed what is now III. 1. 5.

Calas, unjustly condemned at Toulouse in 1762 to torture and execution for the alleged murder of his son. Calas was a Calvinist. His eldest son converted to Roman Catholicism in order to be eligible to practise as an advocate, but was then smitten by remorse and committed suicide. The father was accused of murdering the son, was found guilty despite the lack of any reliable evidence, and was executed on 10 March 1762. Voltaire campaigned vigorously for a re-examination of the case, and a new trial on 9 March 1765 overturned the previous verdict and declared Calas innocent. Any educated European would have heard of the case from the prolonged advocacy of Calas's innocence by Voltaire; but Adam Smith knew more than that. He spent eighteen months at Toulouse in 1764–5 with his pupil, the young Duke of Buccleuch, and must have heard much discussion of the city's *cause célèbre*. He refers to Calas in the course of a virtually new chapter (III. 2) added to the sixth edition of the *Moral Sentiments*, and quotes Calas's last words to the monk who exhorted him to confess: 'My Father, can you yourself bring yourself to believe that I am guilty?' (*TMS* III. 2. 11)

The new chapter distinguishes the love of praise from the love of praiseworthiness and the dread of blame from the dread of blameworthiness. Such a distinction was implicit in the second edition, where the approval and disapproval of actual spectators may be opposed by the judgement of conscience that one does not merit approval or disapproval. But whereas in the second edition Smith had said that the jurisdiction of conscience 'is in a great measure derived from that very tribunal, whose decisions it so often and so justly reverses', in the sixth edition he withdrew that statement and wrote instead: 'The jurisdictions of those two tribunals are founded upon principles which, though in some respects resembling and akin, are, however, in reality different and distinct' (*TMS* III. 2. 32).

He was even ready to reverse the causal relationship in some instances. 'The love of praise-worthiness is by no means derived altogether from the love of praise.' The happiness that we receive from the approval of conscience is confirmed when actual spectators also approve. 'Their praise necessarily strengthens our own sense of our own praise-worthiness. In this case, so far is the love of praise-worthiness from being derived altogether from that of praise; that the love of praise seems, at least in a great measure, to be derived from that of praise-worthiness' (*TMS* III. 2. 2–3).

Adam Smith added some further elaboration of his theory in other new passages written for the sixth edition. As I have noted earlier, he first spoke of the 'impartial' spectator when describing the Stoic virtue of self-command, which he placed on a par with the Christian virtue of love. In the second edition he followed up his reply to Sir Gilbert Elliot's objection with a discussion of the necessity of conscience to counter the force of self-love.[11] The Christian virtue of love or benevolence or humanity, he said, is not strong enough for this purpose. (The words 'benevolence' and 'humanity' suggest an implicit criticism of the theories of Hutcheson and of Hume.) 'It is reason, principle, conscience, the inhabitant of the breast, the man within. . . . It is from him only that we learn the real littleness of ourselves. . . . and the natural misrepresentations of self-love can be corrected only by the eye of this impartial spectator' (*TMS* III. 3. 5).

This function of conscience is closely akin to self-command, and in the sixth edition Smith proceeded in the same chapter to explain the origin and development of self-command in terms of 'that great discipline which Nature has established for the acquisition of this and of every other virtue; a regard to the sentiments of the real or supposed spectator of our conduct' (*TMS* III. 3. 21).

A child, Smith wrote, first learns to control emotion in order to gain the favour and avoid the contempt of his schoolfellows. A man of weak character is like a child; in misfortune he can control his feelings only when others are present. A man of greater firmness remains under the influence of the impartial spectator at all times, so much so that the division of the self into two persons, the imagined spectator and the agent, almost disappears; imagination virtually takes over from reality. 'He almost identifies himself with, he almost becomes himself that impartial spectator, and scarce even feels but

---

[11] To be found, with some revision, at III. 3. 3–5 of the 6th edn.

as that great arbiter of his conduct directs him to feel' (*TMS* iii. 3. 25). But even the most stoical of men cannot altogether escape self-interested feelings in 'paroxysms of distress', such as losing a leg in battle.

He does not, in this case, perfectly identify himself with the ideal man within the breast, he does not become himself the impartial spectator of his own conduct. The different views of both characters exist in his mind separate and distinct from one another, and each directing him to a behaviour different from that to which the other directs him. (*TMS* iii. 3. 28)

Yet agony does not last for ever, and in due course the man who has lost a leg recovers his equanimity. He identifies himself again with 'the ideal man within the breast' and no longer laments his loss. 'The view of the impartial spectator becomes so perfectly habitual to him, that, without any effort, without any exertion, he never thinks of surveying his misfortune in any other view' (*TMS* iii. 3. 29).

Here, as elsewhere, Smith distinguished the impartial 'supposed' spectator from the 'real' one. The rudimentary stage of the virtue of self-command, found in the child or the man of weak character, depends on the feelings of actual spectators. The higher stage, reached by the man of 'constancy and firmness', depends entirely on conscience. What is new in this passage is the view that the agent can identify himself with the imagined spectator to the extent of obliterating the natural feelings of self-regard.

Smith returned to self-command in a later section also added in the sixth edition, and here he wrote of two different standards of moral judgement concerning ourselves. 'The one is the idea of exact propriety and perfection. . . . The other is that degree of approximation to this idea which is commonly attained in the world, and which the greater part of our friends and companions, of our rivals and competitors, may have actually arrived at' (*TMS* vi. iii. 23). The first is the judgement of the impartial spectator. 'There exists in the mind of every man, an idea of this kind, gradually formed from his observations upon the character and conduct both of himself and of other people. It is the slow, gradual, and progressive work of the great demigod within the breast, the great judge and arbiter of conduct' (*TMS* vi. iii. 25). The second standard is reached from observing the actual behaviour of most people.

Smith's distinction in this passage between two standards of judgement is not quite the same as the earlier distinction between the judgement of conscience and that of actual spectators, for the second standard discussed here is derived from the practice of others, not from their reaction as spectators of practice. Still, this distinction is like the earlier one in contrasting the normative ideals of conscience with the positive facts of social life.

Throughout the development of Smith's concept of the impartial spectator his fundamental position was unchanged. In the first edition he stressed the effect of social situation more than the work of the imagination; in the second and the sixth editions he reversed the emphasis: but both were elements in his theory at all stages. Even before he came to draw any sharp contrast between the man within and the man without, Smith's view was that an agent can judge his own character and conduct only if he imagines *himself* in the position of a spectator. And even in his latest thoughts on self-command added to the sixth edition, Smith wrote of 'a regard to the sentiments of the *real or supposed* spectator of our conduct' and said that the child and the man of weak character acquire self-control from adjusting their feelings to those of actual spectators.[12]

---

[12] This chapter has concentrated upon the most important feature of Smith's notion of the impartial spectator, its role in his theory of conscience as an imagined spectator. To avoid misunderstanding, I should perhaps note here that he does also use the term in the more mundane sense of an actual spectator of the conduct of other persons.

6

Comparisons and Comment

Adam Smith's *Moral Sentiments* has naturally been discussed by a number of commentators. In Chapter 1 I have referred to seven of them in connection with differences between the first and the sixth editions of the book. In this chapter I want to consider the thought of two other scholars, Roderick Firth and John Rawls, in connection with the specific notion of the impartial spectator. Before doing so, however, I ought to note that Smith's moral philosophy as a whole has been the subject of attention in the work of yet other scholars, notably Gilbert Harman and Martha Nussbaum. Harman spoke of Smith's book in a much-lauded public lecture, 'Moral Agent and Impartial Spectator', delivered at the University of Kansas in 1986. He expressed the view, which I share, that in ethics Adam Smith is ahead of Hume. Martha Nussbaum, in her book *Love's Knowledge* (1990), has an extensive section on Smith's treatment of the passions when she considers love and the moral point of view, and she again refers to Smith more briefly in a later book, *Upheavals of Thought* (2001).

I have no reason to dissent from the views of those two scholars; indeed Martha Nussbaum's thoughts on Smith are as enlightening as they are novel. I do, however, have some critical remarks on Roderick Firth and John Rawls. Firth proposed an interpretation of moral judgements in terms of an 'ideal observer', which, understandably enough, came to be compared with Adam Smith's theory of the impartial spectator. Rawls is especially worthy of attention because he treated Smith's theory as a rival to his own theory of justice, which has become a classic element in the history of political thought. In his important book *A Theory of Justice*, Rawls wrote of the impartial spectator as a device of utilitarian theory for regarding the interest of society as if it were the interest of a single person.

The aim of Firth's suggestion was to give a 'naturalistic' definition of moral terms such as 'right' and 'wrong': that is to say, a definition that replaced them by words or expressions referring to something observable.[1] This would avoid the idea that moral terms imply the existence of some metaphysical entities beyond the natural world observed by the senses. Firth's suggestion was that a statement of the form 'X is P', where P was 'some particular ethical predicate', could be analysed as having the same meaning as the statement 'Any ideal observer would react to X in such and such a way'. The relevant reaction would commonly be a feeling of approval or disapproval.

Differences between Firth's ideal observer and Adam Smith's impartial spectator were well brought out by my former colleague Tom Campbell in his book *Adam Smith's Science of Morals*. Firth's hypothetical observer is ideal in being omniscient, omnipercipient, disinterested, and dispassionate. As Campbell said, this theory makes the observer more like a god than a man.[2] Adam Smith's impartial spectator is disinterested, but neither omniscient nor omnipercipient, and he is certainly not dispassionate. He has the normal feelings of a normal human being. He approves and disapproves according to his sympathy or lack of sympathy with the feelings of agents and of people affected by action. So far as judgements about others are concerned, Adam Smith's spectator simply is any normal observer who is not personally affected.

But what of the later development of Smith's theory when dealing with judgements about ourselves? What of the description in the second edition of 'this abstract man, the representative of mankind, and substitute of the Deity', or of the phrases used in the sixth edition,

---

[1] Roderick Firth, 'Ethical Absolutism and the Ideal Observer', *Philosophy and Phenomenological Research*, 12 (1952), 317–45.
[2] Campbell, *Adam Smith's Science of Morals*, 133.

the 'ideal' man or 'demigod' within the breast? There is an element of rhetoric here, designed to emphasize the superior authority of conscience when opposing the judgement of actual spectators. The impartial spectator is still a man, not a god, and indeed a perfectly normal man. The 'substitute of the Deity' in the second edition is also 'the representative of mankind'. The metaphorical 'demigod' or 'ideal man within the breast' of the sixth edition is given a clearer interpretation in another late passage added to that edition, where Smith wrote of the 'approbation of the impartial spectator, and of the representative of the impartial spectator, the man within the breast' (*TMS* vi. i. 11). The man within is 'ideal' because he seeks to be praiseworthy more than to be actually praised by 'the man without'. The judgement of conscience is superior to that of actual spectators simply because the agent can know better than bystanders what he has done or not done, and what was his motive for acting as he did. He is 'well-informed' but he is not omniscient. His superior knowledge is a matter of common experience.

If the man without should applaud us, either for actions which we have not performed, or for motives which had no influence upon us; the man within can immediately humble that pride and elevation of mind which such groundless acclamations might otherwise occasion, by telling us, that as we know we do not deserve them, we render ourselves despicable by accepting them. If, on the contrary, the man without should reproach us, either for actions which we never performed, or for motives which had no influence upon those which we may have performed; the man within may immediately correct this false judgment, and assure us, that we are by no means the proper object of that censure which has so unjustly been bestowed upon us. (*TMS* iii. 2. 32)[3]

For John Rawls the concept of the impartial spectator was a device of utilitarian theory. 'Endowed with ideal powers of sympathy and imagination, the impartial spectator is the perfectly rational individual who identifies with and experiences the desires of others

---

[3] Added in the 6th edn.

as if these desires were his own.'[4] He can thus organize the interests of society into a single system of self-interested desires that everyone constructs for himself. In working out this notion Rawls was probably influenced more by Hume than by Adam Smith, though he describes his account as 'reminiscent' of both these thinkers[5] and includes both in his list of classical utilitarians.[6] It seems likely that Rawls did not pay close attention to Smith's *Moral Sentiments*. In his first reference, a long note on 'classical utilitarians', he misquotes the title of Smith's book as *A Theory of the Moral Sentiments*,[7] and in two subsequent notes he cites the book from selections in other works.[8]

Far from being a utilitarian, Adam Smith was a severe critic of utilitarianism in many parts of his ethics and jurisprudence. He did, of course, write in *The Wealth of Nations* about a natural harmony of individual and social interests, but there he was abstracting economic activity from the whole of social life, and in any event that harmony owed nothing to sympathy. In Smith's theory of approval the spectator's sympathy is concerned first with the motive of the agent. The spectator imagines himself in the shoes of the agent, and if he finds that he would share the agent's feelings, the correspondence of sentiments constitutes his 'sympathy' (as Smith used the term) and causes him to approve the agent's motive as right and proper. In some circumstances a second species of sympathy may be added to this first one. If the agent's action benefits another person, the spectator may find that he sympathizes with the beneficiary's gratitude as well as with the agent's benevolence. This double sympathy causes the

---

[4] John Rawls, *A Theory of Justice* (Cambridge, Mass.: Harvard University Press, 1971; Oxford: Clarendon Press, 1972), 27. In the rev. edn. of 1999 the passage appears unaltered on pp. 23–4. I corresponded with Rawls in 1973 about his representation of Adam Smith's position. He conceded that he was mistaken in failing to distinguish between the views of Hume and Smith, and he said that he would try to correct the error 'if there is ever a second edition'. No doubt he had forgotten about this when he prepared the revised edition.

[5] Ibid. 184 (rev. edn. 161).　　　[6] Ibid. 22 (rev. edn. 20), n. 9.　　　[7] Ibid.

[8] Ibid. 184 (rev. edn. 161), n. 34, cites *TMS* from the extracts in L. A. Selby-Bigge (ed.), *British Moralists* (Oxford: Clarendon Press, 1897). Ibid. 479 (rev. edn. 419), n. 16, cites a passage of *TMS* from the selections in H. W. Schneider (ed.), *Adam Smith's Moral and Political Philosophy* (New York: Hafner, 1948).

spectator to approve of the action as meritorious. Smith agreed with Hume that utility pleases a spectator through sympathy with the pleasure given to the person or persons benefited, but he entirely disagreed with Hume's view that this kind of sympathetic pleasure is the sole or main constituent of moral approval. In his final account of the matter Smith listed four grounds or 'sources' of moral approval, and made a regard to utility the last and the least of these.

When we approve of any character or action, the sentiments which we feel, are . . . derived from four sources . . . First, we sympathize with the motives of the agent; secondly, we enter into the gratitude of those who receive the benefit of his actions; thirdly, we observe that his conduct has been agreeable to the general rules by which those two sympathies generally act; and, last of all, when we consider such actions as making a part of a system of behaviour which tends to promote the happiness either of the individual or of the society, they appear to derive a beauty from this utility, not unlike that which we ascribe to any well-contrived machine. (*TMS* vii. iii. 3. 16)

What sort of thing was Adam Smith's theory of the impartial spectator meant to be, and what was it meant to do? It was meant to be a sociological and psychological explanation of some moral capacities. That is not a task that any modern philosopher would take on; but philosophical theories continue to be rather odd, and it is as well to recognize the glass houses of the modern counterparts before throwing stones at Adam Smith's construction.

Roderick Firth proposed his ideal observer theory as an analysis of the *meaning* of moral judgements, and as such it is simply incredible. The suggestion is that when you or I say that an action is right, we mean, we intend to assert, that it would evoke a favourable reaction in an observer who was omniscient, omnipercipient, disinterested, and dispassionate. We have all been making moral judgements happily (or unhappily) from early youth, but it is a safe bet that none of us had the remotest thought of connecting them with an omniscient and dispassionate observer until we heard of it from Firth's philosophical theory.

John Rawls was doing something different. He presented the impartial spectator version of utilitarianism as a possible alternative to his own, contractual, theory of justice. He did not regard either theory as an analysis of meaning. Rather he thought of them as hypotheses of what (logically) could have produced our present thoughts, though he did not for a moment suppose that either of these possible causes was an actual cause. Like Hobbes,[9] Rawls evidently thought that one can explain something by reasoning from known effects to *possible* causes. Such a procedure may improve our understanding of a problem, but it is misleading if used to interpret the theory of an earlier philosopher.

Adam Smith did not anticipate either of these modern theorists. He was certainly not giving an analysis of the meaning of moral judgements,[10] nor was he putting forward a hypothesis of a purely *possible* cause. He was presenting a hypothesis of the actual causal process whereby judgements of conscience are formed. Today we would regard this as a scientific rather than a philosophical function. Fortunately the division of labour had not been carried that far in Adam Smith's time.

Adam Smith's theory can certainly stand comparison with the best known of modern psychological explanations of conscience, Freud's account of the super-ego. This is similar to Smith's view in taking conscience to be a second self built up in the mind as a reflection of the attitudes of outside persons. Freud's hypothesis is presumably helpful in the diagnosis and treatment of certain neuroses. But, if regarded as a general theory of the formation of conscience, normal as well as abnormal, it is less satisfactory than Adam Smith's account because it takes too narrow a view of the causal agencies. Freud concentrated (though not exclusively) on the attitude of parents, while Adam Smith thought of the reaction of society in general and mentioned the influence of teachers and schoolfellows as well as parents when referring to the growth of conscience in children.

---

[9] Thomas Hobbes, *Leviathan* (1651), ch. 46, first sentence.

[10] Smith does, incautiously, say at the end of *TMS* III. 5. 5: 'The very words, right, wrong, fit, improper, graceful, unbecoming, mean only what pleases or displeases those [i.e. moral] faculties.' The passage is, I suggest a little later in this chapter, part of an early version of his lectures.

A more important difference is that Freud emphasized the negative attitudes of disapproval, on the one side, and fear of punishment, on the other, and so he represented the super-ego as predominantly (though again not exclusively) a restrictive or censorious element in the mind. He accounted for the excessively rigid conscience produced by a repressive upbringing, but not for the more liberal kind produced by an affectionate upbringing. Adam Smith, unlike Freud, did not stress the force of disapproval and fear. He spoke of both favourable and unfavourable attitudes on the part of society as having a place in the formation of conscience.

What was Smith's theory meant to do? It was meant to provide a satisfactory alternative to rationalist a priori accounts of conscience and morality generally. Like Hutcheson and Hume before him, Smith was a good empiricist. All three aimed at giving an explanation of ethics in terms of 'human nature'—empirical psychology, we would say today. But Smith appreciated that the theories of Hutcheson and Hume were inadequate to account for the peculiarities of conscience. Hutcheson in his later years accepted Bishop Butler's description of the 'authority' of conscience, but without explaining how this could be fitted into the moral sense theory. At first Adam Smith followed the example of his teacher Hutcheson in endorsing Butler. There is one passage in the *Moral Sentiments* where Smith wrote as if he were unconsciously quoting Butler, even to the extent of inferring divine intention from the character of moral judgement.

Upon whatever we suppose that our moral faculties are founded, whether upon a certain modification of reason, upon an original instinct, called a moral sense, or upon some other principle of our nature, it cannot be doubted, that they were given us for the direction of our conduct in this life. They carry along with them the most evident badges of this authority.... Since these, therefore, were plainly intended to be the governing principles of human nature, the rules which they prescribe are to be regarded as the commands and laws of the Deity, promulgated by those vicegerents which he has thus set up within us. (*TMS* III. 5. 5–6)

This passage inevitably recalls familiar phrases of Bishop Butler: 'upon supposition of such a moral faculty; whether called conscience, moral reason, moral sense, or divine reason';[11] 'conscience ... plainly bears upon it marks of authority over all the rest, and claims the absolute direction of them all'.[12]

Smith's passage probably formed part of an early version of his lectures on moral philosophy: it includes a statement that the moral faculties 'may be considered as a sort of senses', a statement that is not consistent with his criticism elsewhere of Hutcheson's moral sense theory. If I am right, the early version of Smith's lectures was written before he had developed his own theory of conscience. In due course he came to see (no doubt influenced by Hume) that the use of empirical method required one to explain, not just to assert, the existence of peculiar qualities. Hutcheson had not been empirical enough in regarding the moral sense as an original endowment of human nature; and Butler had not been empirical enough in taking the authority of conscience to be a simple datum, intelligible only by reference to theology. An empirical account could go further: both phenomena, the moral sense and its character of authority, could be explained as the natural effects of ordinary experience, notably in the use of imagination.

In evaluating Adam Smith's theory, the first question that arises is whether Smith, any more than Butler, remained true to the empirical method. He wanted to explain ethics in terms of empirical psychology and sociology, yet he ended up with the apparently conventional thesis that moral rules are equivalent to divine laws and that conscience has an authority superior to social approval and disapproval. The reader is apt to think that about halfway through the book Smith abandoned empiricism and slipped into the traditional views of theologians and rationalists without noticing the inconsistency. A more careful scrutiny of his theory shows that this is not so. His concept of the impartial spectator remained empirical throughout, as I hope will be clear from my report of it. We shall

[11] Joseph Butler, 'Dissertation of the Nature of Virtue', appended to *The Analogy of Religion* (1736), §2.
[12] Butler, *Fifteen Sermons*, preface, §18.

see in the next chapter that the same thing is true of Smith's account of moral rules, an account that is no less ingenious, but perhaps less impressive, than his theory of conscience.

A second question that arises is whether it is reasonable to attribute greater complexity to moral judgements made about ourselves than to those made about others. If Smith had been giving an analysis of meaning, this would be a fair criticism. There is no reason to suppose that the statement 'I ought to shut up' has a more complicated meaning than the statement 'You ought to shut up'. Smith's theory does not have that implication. His view was that the first statement has a more complicated history.

Still, if he were right, might we not expect to see some traces of a difference of character between first-person moral judgements and the rest? Well, there is one respect in which we do differentiate between them. We not only recognize that an agent's judgement about himself may be independent of the judgement of others about him. We also accept the principle that it is a person's moral duty to follow his or her conscience even though it may be misguided. I think that some moral theorists exaggerate the scope of this principle, treating it as applicable to all situations, regardless of the rights of other people who are affected by the action concerned. Experience leads me to believe that our respect for the following of conscience is queried when the conscientious action breaches a definite right of someone else. But, allowing for some reservation on that score, we do generally think that the judgement of conscience in directing one's own conduct should have priority over the judgement made by other people. This fact does nothing to confirm Adam Smith's particular theory, but it does rebut the suggestion that an account of moral judgements concerning ourselves should be on all fours with an account of moral judgements concerning others.

Finally, however, I wish to pose a criticism of a different kind about the complexity of Adam Smith's hypothesis. It seems to me that his concept of the impartial spectator is too complicated to be acceptable when one works it out fully in terms of his general theory of approval. On Smith's view, an ordinary spectator approves of an agent's conduct if he finds, after imagining himself in the agent's shoes, that he would feel and act as the agent does. An agent who consults his conscience in judging his own conduct has to imagine himself in the position of an uninvolved spectator while retaining his present knowledge of the facts. He has to imagine that he is an uninvolved spectator who in turn imagines himself to be in the position of the involved agent; and, having performed this feat of imagination doubling back on its tracks, the agent has to ask himself whether the feelings that he imagines he would then experience do or do not correspond to the feelings that he actually experiences now. The process is not impossible but it seems too complicated to be a common experience.

W. R. Scott once suggested that Adam Smith had exceptional powers of imagination himself and 'as a Moral Philosopher he insisted on crediting everyone with his own genius'.[13] That too is not impossible but again unlikely if only because the quoted words imply that Smith was rather unimaginative in his social observation. I prefer to think that Smith, like anyone else, could make a mistake in the details of his theory. The difficulty that I have described becomes apparent only when one spells out Smith's theory of conscience in terms of his theory of approval. The idea of the impartial spectator seems persuasive when taken by itself, with an unanalysed notion of approval. This suggests that the trouble lies in Smith's initial theory of approval, the defects of which were shown in earlier chapters of this book.

[13] W. R. Scott, *Adam Smith: An Oration* (Glasgow: Glasgow University Publications, No. 48, 1938), 11.

7

Moral Rules

Adam Smith's view of moral rules is connected with his view of conscience. I said in the last chapter that on a first reading one is apt to think there is an inconsistency between Smith's initial aim and the eventual result: his aim was to explain ethics in terms of empirical psychology and sociology, yet he ended up with the conventional thesis of rationalists and theologians that moral rules are divine laws. It is not easy to decide whether the inconsistency is real or apparent. Is the end result Smith's own view, or is he simply showing how the conventional view (of people generally, reflected in rationalist philosophy) comes about, without implying that he himself shares it?

I am inclined to think that he does share the conventional view and that he could give an argument for accepting it, namely that, since the process of coming to accept the conventional view is *natural*, it is proper to go along with it. This would mean that Smith is a theoretical sceptic and a pragmatic conformist. I have to admit, however, that Smith himself does not give us the suggested argument. Maybe he was not explicitly aware of it, or of the apparent inconsistency in his discussion.

Smith discusses moral rules in two different places. In the sixth edition of the *Moral Sentiments* the first discussion is to be found in part III, chapters 4 and 5, while the second discussion is in part VII, section iii, chapter 2.

The first discussion is more elaborate than the second and includes what I have called the end result. Chapter 4 of part III describes the 'origin' of general rules, namely inductive reasoning, while chapter 5 is entitled 'Of the influence and authority of the general Rules of

Morality, and that they are justly regarded as the Laws of the Deity'. The content of chapter 4 includes some material that was not in the first edition, but on the topic of general rules there is no significant change.

The second discussion, the chapter in part VII, is, apart from a couple of trifles, identical with the corresponding chapter (part VI, section iii, chapter 2) in the first edition. It recalls the more elaborate discussion of part III but is confined to describing the origin of moral rules in inductive reasoning. I have noted in my first chapter that this final part of the *Moral Sentiments* seems to me to come from the beginning of Smith's course of lectures at Glasgow.

Chapter 4 of part III leads into the topic of general rules after a discussion of the dangers of self-deceit from inevitable partiality towards our own interest. Smith suggests that nature leads us to form general moral rules in order to guard against such self-deceit. He then explains how the general rules are formed: they arise, he says, from our reaction to the conduct, especially the shocking conduct, of *other people*. Awareness of one's own reaction is reinforced by seeing that everyone else is affected in the same way, and also, of course, by seeing that the particular kind of reaction is repeated whenever one encounters the particular kind of conduct. For example, we are shocked whenever we see or hear of a murder, motivated by some such motive as avarice or envy.

We resolve never to be guilty of the like, nor ever, upon any account, to render ourselves in this manner the objects of universal disapprobation. We thus naturally lay down to ourselves a general rule, that all such actions are to be avoided, as tending to render us odious, contemptible, or punishable, the objects of all those sentiments for which we have the greatest dread and aversion.

On the other hand, conduct that provokes a reaction of approval leads to 'a rule of another kind, that every opportunity of acting in this manner is carefully to be sought after' (*TMS* III. 4. 7).

Smith then proceeds to spell out the logic of the process, an aspect that he emphasizes still further in the later discussion of part VII.

In that later discussion he explicitly uses the term 'induction' on more than one occasion. He does not do so here in part III, but induction is clearly what he has in mind. He says that the general rules are 'founded upon experience of what, in particular instances, our moral faculties, our natural sense of merit and propriety, approve, or disapprove of' (*TMS* III. 4. 8). The chief point that he wants to make is that the general rules depend upon initial particular judgements, as contrasted with the view of philosophical rationalists that all particular moral judgements depend upon their conformity to general rules. It is easy to suppose that the rationalists' view is true, because we often do reach a particular moral judgement by reference to a general rule; but this, Smith argues, can be done only when the general rules have been established, and the process of establishing general rules displays the priority of making moral judgements in particular cases.

When we do appeal to general rules in order to reach a judgement, Smith says, it is usually when we are 'debating concerning the degree of praise or blame that is due to certain actions of a complicated and dubious nature' (*TMS* III. 4. 11). What does that mean? In what circumstances would one debate about the *degree* of praise or blame? And in what way is an *action* complicated and dubious? I must suppose that Smith is thinking of moral dilemmas, the need to choose when two or more moral notions are involved and there is a conflict between them. A simple example: I am asked a question, and I know that a straightforwardly true answer, if passed on to others, would cause pain to some of those others. I might then 'debate' with myself whether, or how far, it would be blameworthy to give the true answer without qualification, and also how far it would be blameworthy to give a false answer or to refuse to answer. Allotting degrees of blame implies allotting also degrees of praise to the converse possibilities.

In such situations of moral debate, Smith agrees, we are indeed thinking about general rules that we have already acquired, and we 'appeal to them as to the standards of judgment'. Smith believes this has misled the rationalist philosophers into thinking that 'the original judgments of mankind with regard to right and wrong were formed like the decisions of a court of judicatory', which proceeds by first considering a general rule and then asking whether the particular action brought before it falls under that rule.

Smith concedes, notably in the later discussion of part VII, that it is proper to say that virtue 'consists in a conformity to reason' because the general rules are reached by reason, inductive reasoning (*TMS* VII. iii. 2. 6). But, he goes on, it is 'altogether absurd and unintelligible to suppose that the first perceptions of right and wrong can be derived from reason'. His argument for this assertion is a repetition of what Hume had written on the subject.

These first perceptions . . . cannot be the object of reason, but of immediate sense and feeling. It is by finding in a vast variety of instances that one tenor of conduct constantly pleases in a certain manner, and that another as constantly displeases the mind, that we form the general rules of morality. But reason cannot render any particular object either agreeable or disagreeable to the mind for its own sake. Reason may show that this object is the means of obtaining some other which is naturally either pleasing or displeasing, and in this manner may render it either agreeable or disagreeable for the sake of something else. But nothing can be agreeable or disagreeable for its own sake, which is not rendered such by immediate sense and feeling. (*TMS* iii. 2. 7)[1]

In part III Smith adds the more provocative thesis that the general rules of morality are commands and laws of God, who will reward obedience and punish breach of these laws. Smith says that this belief 'is first impressed by nature, and afterwards confirmed by reasoning and philosophy' (*TMS* III. 5. 3). He then elaborates his view of the two processes.

The initial 'impression by nature' is a primitive religious belief. All human beings 'are naturally led' to think of their gods as being like themselves. So they ascribe to the gods their own feelings (together

---

[1] Cf. Hume, *Treatise of Human Nature*, III. i. 1–2. Smith's phrase, 'pleases in a certain manner', recalls Hume, *Treatise*, III. ii. 5, 'when any action, or quality of the mind, pleases us *after a certain manner*, we say it is virtuous'.

with a greater power than men possess to give effect to those feelings). The gods would therefore share human attitudes towards behaviour: they would approve of 'humanity and mercy' as worthy of reward, and they would disapprove of 'perfidy and injustice' as worthy of being avenged. 'And thus religion, even in its rudest form, gave a sanction to the rules of morality, long before the age of artificial reasoning and philosophy.' Such measures were necessary for 'the happiness of mankind' and too important for that purpose to have to wait upon 'the slowness and uncertainty of philosophical researches' (*TMS* III. 5. 4).

The 'philosophical researches' that follow consist of three arguments. The first of them echoes notable phrases used by Bishop Butler and the second could be the elaboration of a hint in Butler; but the third is different, clearly foreshadowing Adam Smith the economist. All three arguments appear in the first edition of the *Moral Sentiments* and continue unchanged in the subsequent editions. The first argument, however, contains an indication of coming from an early version of Smith's lectures, and that may not be true of the other two. The indication is the statement (already mentioned in Chapter 6) that the moral faculties 'may be considered as a sort of senses', a remark inconsistent with Smith's criticism of Hutcheson's moral sense theory at two other places in the book.

I draw attention to this point because the whole passage about 'philosophical researches' seems to me to betray some uneasiness about theology on Smith's part. After giving his first argument, plainly drawn from a confident Bishop Butler, Smith precedes each of his other arguments by telling us that there are *many* such: 'There are innumerable other considerations which serve to confirm the same conclusion.' 'There are besides many other reasons, and many other natural principles, which all tend to confirm and inculcate the same salutary doctrine' (*TMS* III. 5. 7–8). He cannot be expected to spell out 'innumerable' arguments, and maybe we should be satisfied with two as a fair sample. Still, it is rather odd to *repeat* that there are many when you are giving only two. We shall see in a later chapter that Smith did come to be hesitant about his theological beliefs, and perhaps this is presaged by the uneasiness that I find in the passage about moral rules.

The first of the three arguments is that our 'moral faculties' carry 'badges' of authority, showing that they were 'given us', 'were set up within us' to be 'supreme arbiters' of action, to 'superintend' our feelings and desires. They are therefore to be regarded as commands and laws of God. The name of 'law' is applied to all general rules, including those of natural science (as in 'the laws of nature'), but the rules of morality have a greater resemblance than other general rules to laws proper.

This is not wholly drawn from Butler: Smith's final point, that the term 'law' is more apt for ethics than for natural science, is his own addition. But the initial statement of the argument recalls Butler's actual words as well as his thought. Butler says that conscience 'plainly bears upon it marks of authority' and that 'you cannot form a notion of this faculty, conscience, without taking in judgment, direction, superintendency'.[2]

Smith's argument is intended to be an appeal to general experience. What experience is referred to by the term 'badges of authority'? Smith explains it by pointing to a distinction between our 'moral faculties' and 'the other faculties of our nature'.

No other faculty or principle of action judges of any other. Love does not judge of resentment, nor resentment of love. Those two passions may be opposite to one another, but cannot, with any propriety, be said to approve or disapprove of one another. But it is the peculiar office of those faculties now under our consideration to judge, to bestow censure or applause upon all the other principles of our nature. They may be considered as a sort of senses of which those principles are the objects. Every sense is supreme over its own objects. There is no appeal from the eye with regard to the beauty of colours, nor from the ear with regard to the harmony of sounds, nor from the taste with regard to the agreeableness of flavours. Each of those senses judges in the last resort of its own objects. . . . It belongs to our moral faculties, in the same manner to determine when the ear ought to be

---

[2] Butler, *Fifteen Sermons*, preface, §18, and sermon ii, §19.

soothed, when the eye ought to be indulged, when the taste ought to be gratified, when and how far every other principle of our nature ought either to be indulged or restrained. What is agreeable to our moral faculties, is fit, and right, and proper to be done; the contrary wrong, unfit, and improper. (*TMS* III. 5. 5)

The analogy with the senses is, of course, imperfect. Each of the three senses named by Smith operates by means of a bodily organ, and that applies also to smell—and to touch with the proviso that the bodily medium for touch can be any part of the skin. What Smith calls the 'moral faculties' is the capacity for making moral judgements, and that does not operate through a bodily medium. We should recognize, however, that what he here calls a sense—the eye, the ear, and the taste—is not simply perception through a bodily organ or medium: it includes judgement. He writes of the eye judging the beauty of colours, not simply of perceiving colours; and likewise of the ear judging the harmony of sounds, not simply of hearing sounds. These are aesthetic judgements (though one cannot say that of judging the 'agreeableness' of flavours). Smith's analogy between moral judgement and the senses is, strictly speaking, an analogy with aesthetic (or quasi-aesthetic) judgement about the data supplied by the senses. We should, therefore, not dismiss his first argument as relying on an inadequate analogy.

What, then, are we to make of his description of the function of moral judgement, 'to determine when the ear ought to be soothed, when the eye ought to be indulged, when the taste ought to be gratified'? He cannot mean that moral judgement acts as a censor of the ear's judgement of the harmony of sounds, or the eye's judgement of the beauty of colours, or the taste's judgement of the pleasure of flavours. He must mean that it censors the exercise of sight, hearing, and eating even if they are accompanied by a positive aesthetic judgement.

What is the argument trying to prove? It claims that the capacity to make moral judgements is superior to other human capacities because it includes critical judgements on them, whereas every one of those other capacities is confined to judgements within its own sphere. The evidence for this contention is that the moral capacity expresses approval and disapproval of the deliverances of other capacities: it determines when and how far the others 'ought either to be indulged or restrained'. What sort of thing does Smith have in mind? In what circumstances would the moral capacity judge that we ought not to see, hear, taste, smell, or touch what the relevant sense finds beautiful, harmonious, savoury, or tactually pleasurable? It would have to be a situation where the positive aesthetic character is accompanied by a negative ethical character. Such situations are not very common. An example for vision might be watching the skilful planning and carrying-out of a crime. An example for taste might be eating more of an enjoyable food than is your fair share at a communal meal.

It is probable, however, that Smith is not restricting his thought so narrowly. Although he describes the senses as delivering aesthetic judgements, he is probably thinking simply of sense-perception when he says that conscience has the wide power of judging the exercise of all the senses. If you asked for examples, he might instance moral disapproval of reading pornography, or looking at private papers without permission, listening to malicious gossip, tasting what is literally forbidden fruit, amorously kissing your neighbour's wife.

In any event his argument is flawed. It depends on assigning to conscience the exclusive function of judging what ought and what ought not to be done. That function is not exclusive to conscience but is exercised also by prudential self-interest. My example for the moral censorship of taste was the judgement that you ought not to eat more than your *fair share* of an enjoyable food at a communal meal. A similar censorship is exercised by prudential reason, which will tell you that you ought not to eat more of an enjoyable food than is *good for you*.

The similarity between conscience and prudence is occasionally acknowledged in Bishop Butler's analysis of the leading motives in human nature: he calls prudence 'cool' or 'reasonable' self-love and is prepared to say that 'reasonable self-love and conscience are the chief or superior principles in the nature of man',[3] even though he more often writes as if conscience were the sole 'principle of reflection'. He tries to maintain the higher status of conscience by saying that cool self-love is concerned only with maximizing happiness in earthly life while conscience takes account also of life in the world to come.

Smith seems unaware of the difficulty posed by prudence. It might be suggested that his use of the plural term 'our moral faculties' perhaps refers to prudence as well as to conscience, but there is no evidence of that. When he first introduces the term 'moral faculties', he explains it as 'our natural sense of merit and propriety', and I think he uses the plural form to encompass these two forms of moral judgement. He calls prudence a virtue, that is, a possible object of positive moral judgement; but he does not write of prudence as itself a form of moral judgement. I conclude that we must reject as faulty Smith's first philosophical argument for the thesis that moral rules are laws of God.

His second argument is theological and teleological. God's purpose in creating mankind must have been to make them happy. This follows from the wisdom and beneficence that we necessarily ascribe to him as a perfect being, and it is confirmed by observation of the works of nature, which generally promote happiness and 'guard against' misery. When we follow the dictates of moral judgement, we are taking the most effective means to the end of promoting human happiness, and so we are co-operating with God and contributing to his aim. Action to the contrary is obstructing the divine plan and declaring ourselves the enemies of God. We can hope for reward in the former case and must expect punishment in the latter.

The argument is based on self-interest and assumes that an appeal to this motive is the best, or the most likely, way to induce us to obey the rules of morality. No doubt it is effective for people who are ready to accept the underlying theological doctrine.

The third argument is more interesting and certainly more original. Smith claims that the natural consequences of virtuous action

---

[3] Butler, *Fifteen Sermons*, sermon iii, §13.

generally have the character of recompense for work, thereby encouraging and promoting its repetition. For example, 'industry, prudence, and circumspection' normally produce success in any enterprise, and that success encourages the continuance of the beneficial efforts; 'the practice of truth, justice, and humanity' gains the confidence and esteem of our neighbours, which in turn encourages the continued practice of those virtues. Smith admits that there are exceptions. Unlucky circumstances may cause a good man to be wrongly suspected of a crime and to be reviled 'for the remaining part of his life'. A person who practises caution and circumspection may be ruined by the exceptional occurrence of an earthquake or flood. But these exceptions are rare. If an innocent man is wrongly suspected of a crime, his well-known integrity is likely to make people disbelieve the charges against him. Likewise a knave may sometimes manage to dress up a knavish action so as to appear faultless or even good; but generally his habitual knavery will make people think ill of him even when he happens to have done nothing wrong (*TMS* III. 5. 8).

Yet, despite this natural occurrence of a just distribution of prosperity and adversity, our common moral sentiments are often dissatisfied. There are some virtues and vices that affect our feelings so strongly that we want to see the natural rewards and punishments increased. We admire the moral virtues of 'magnanimity, generosity, and justice' so highly that we would like to see them rewarded with wealth, power, and honours, benefits that are, in the natural course of things, the appropriate rewards for the economic virtues of prudence and industry. Similarly we detest 'fraud, falsehood, brutality, and violence' so much that we are indignant if a knave who exhibits them also happens to be industrious and benefits from his industry.

Both the economic tendencies and the common moral sentiments are products of nature, so that nature is inconsistent. Smith does not seem to be worried about this. He says that laws are enacted to modify the natural economic process and bring it more into line with moral sentiment.

Thus man is by Nature directed to correct, in some measure, that distribution of things which she herself would otherwise have made. The rules which for this purpose she prompts him to follow, are different from those which she herself observes. She bestows upon every virtue, and upon every vice, that precise reward or punishment which is best fitted to encourage the one, or to restrain the other. She is directed by this sole consideration, and pays little regard to the different degrees of merit and demerit, which they may seem to possess in the sentiments and passions of man. Man, on the contrary, pays regard to this [i.e. merit] only...The rules which she follows are fit for her, those which he follows for him: but both are calculated to promote the same great end, the order of the world, and the perfection and happiness of human nature. (*TMS* iii. 5. 9)

The possibilities of 'correcting' the natural economic process are limited, so that men feel frustrated as well as indignant. In their despair they 'naturally appeal to heaven' and hope that God will put things right 'in a life to come'. Thus the general rules about the merit and demerit of actions 'come to be regarded as the laws of an All-powerful Being, who . . . will reward the observance, and punish the breach of them' (*TMS* iii. 5. 10, 12).

As I said at the beginning of this chapter, it is not altogether clear whether Smith intends simply to explain how the theological belief arises or whether he shares it. He says here that the general rules 'come to be regarded' as divine laws, and he then goes on to say: 'That our regard to the will of the Deity ought to be the supreme rule of our conduct, can be doubted of by nobody who believes his existence.' Smith himself certainly believed in the existence of God, but these words evidently allow for doubters (such as his friend Hume). As for his own position, although he abandoned Christian doctrine in his maturity, he seems to have retained a belief in natural religion. In a letter of 15 October 1766, writing of the illness of the Duke of Buccleuch's brother, Smith expressed concern for the boy's mother, using religious language: 'I pray God to preserve and to prepare her for whatever may be the event of this terrible disorder.'[4]

---

[4] *Correspondence of Adam Smith*, 121.

And in part VI of the *Moral Sentiments*, composed in 1788–9, Smith wrote that 'God himself is the immediate administrator and director' of the 'great society of all sensible and intelligent beings' (*TMS* VI. 3. 3).

Coming back to the third argument itself, it lacks cogency as a ground for treating general rules as laws of God. It is, however, an impressive example of Adam Smith's percipience as an observer of human nature.

8

Virtue

In the earlier version of the *Moral Sentiments* there is only a limited discussion of virtue and the primary virtues. Part II contains a short section on justice and beneficence, comparing these two virtues and then giving its chief attention to justice. The final part (VI in this earlier version) is a historical survey, including a section of four chapters on different views of 'the nature of virtue'. In the first three of these chapters we are told of theorists who claim that virtue can be summed up in a single concept: one set goes for propriety (here meaning the 'proper' direction of all feelings); another set goes for prudence, a rational pursuit of self-interest; a third set picks on benevolence, a rational pursuit of the interests of others. The fourth chapter deals with theories that claim virtue to be a sham: it names two thinkers, La Rochefoucauld and Mandeville, going into detail only on the latter. In the sixth edition Smith omitted the brief reference to La Rochefoucauld, thereby fulfilling a promise made, some years earlier, to the contemporary Duc de La Rochefoucauld in a letter acknowledging that Smith's representation of the duke's ancestor was mistaken. That change, however, was a mere trifle; the sixth edition is marked out by a far more radical development in the discussion of virtue.

It consists in the insertion of a whole new part of considerable length, entitled 'Of the Character of Virtue'. This became part VI, and the concluding part, formerly VI, now became VII. I said in Chapter 1 that I think Smith composed this extensive addition to his book because he realized that he had omitted to carry out the whole of his stated programme. He had said that the subject matter of moral philosophy consists of two main topics, the nature of virtue and the nature of moral judgement. Even the extended version of the book in the sixth edition gives far more attention to the second topic, moral judgement, than to the first, the nature of virtue, but the earlier version had said very little indeed about the first topic.

The new part VI divides the virtues into three categories: prudence, which concerns the happiness of oneself; justice and beneficence, which concern the happiness of other people; and self-command, without which no virtue can reach perfection. Prudence, beneficence, and self-command are each treated at length in separate sections. There is no such section for justice. Smith explains the omission in his introduction to the second section (*TMS* VI. ii, intro. 2). In the first place, he says, the principles of positive justice, permitting action that restrains or punishes, are the subject of the 'particular science' of jurisprudence and so need no detailed account in a book on ethics; and, secondly, the general principle of negative justice, forbidding action that hurts or disturbs the happiness of others, is so obvious as to need no further explanation. Smith's first remark, about positive (or legal) justice, probably implies that he had written at length about it in his uncompleted book on jurisprudence (the manuscript of which was destroyed just before his death, in accordance with his wishes). He had also already included a fair amount about the basic concept of justice in part II of the *Moral Sentiments*, where an initial statement of differences between justice and beneficence is followed by discussion of the links between justice and the main topic of part II, merit and demerit. In contrast with this excursus on justice, beneficence and prudence had not received detailed description in the original book but had apparently been taken for granted as virtues that are plainly intelligible.

The new part VI, then, repairs an omission in adding sections on prudence and beneficence. The same thing is true of the section on self-command. Just as the original book had contrasted justice and beneficence, it had likewise emphasized differences between benevolence (or 'humanity') and self-command. This was in part I, section i, chapter 5, 'Of the amiable and respectable virtues'. The language was influenced by Hume, and that is why Smith wrote in this place of 'humanity' rather than 'benevolence' (though he did also write of 'benevolent affections' at one point). His intention was to contrast the Christian virtue of love or benevolence with the Stoic virtue of self-command and to set them up as equal partners in an overall plan of the virtues. I quoted the relevant passage in Chapter 1 above and repeated the crucial sentence in Chapter 5. It gives self-command a cardinal role among the virtues, and when Smith came to elaborate his account of the character of virtue in the new part VI he was bound to highlight self-command as much as beneficence.

In fact self-command is made more prominent still in the sixth edition. It is not only the subject of a section in the added part VI but is also the main topic of a new chapter in part III, 'Of the Influence and Authority of Conscience'. The first part of this new chapter had been added (to the preceding chapter) in the second edition as an answer to Sir Gilbert Elliot's criticism of Smith's view of conscience. But the major part of the new chapter is a disquisition on self-command. One is almost inclined to say that the role of self-command has now become superior to that of Christian love, though this would be going too far. Smith retained the passage that gives equal status to Christian love and Stoic self-command. If he had been asked to rate his cardinal virtues in a relative order of value, I believe he would have said that one cannot assign higher and lower values to justice, beneficence, and self-command. Justice is the essential basis; beneficence and self-command are the apexes; all three are of equal importance.

The same cannot be said of Smith's remaining cardinal virtue, prudence. It is given more prominence than in the earlier version of the book, and the late Professor A. L. Macfie and I were led to say, in our introduction to the *Moral Sentiments*, that this 'increased attention to prudence in edition 6 is natural from the more mature Adam Smith who had pondered on economics for so long' (*TMS*, introduction, *18*). No doubt that is true, but the section on prudence in the new part VI is there to repair an omission, as is the section on beneficence. It does not imply that Smith now valued prudence more highly or that he placed it on a level with justice, beneficence, and self-command. Indeed he explicitly says twice that approval of the self-interested virtue of prudence is limited to 'cold esteem' (*TMS* VI. i. 14; VI, concl. 5).

To be sure, this self-interested virtue is also called the 'inferior' or 'vulgar' (that is, common) form of prudence, as contrasted with a 'superior' prudence that presupposes 'the utmost perfection of all the intellectual and of all the moral virtues' (*TMS* VI. i. 15); but this 'superior prudence' is not a species of the virtue that forms the subject and the title of part VI, section i, prudence as 'the Character of the Individual, so far as it affects his own Happiness'. When Smith writes of 'superior prudence', he is referring to the use of the word 'prudence' to describe wise policy for the public interest. 'Wise and judicious conduct, when directed to greater and nobler purposes than the care of the health, the fortune, the rank and reputation of the individual, is frequently and very properly called prudence. We talk of the prudence of the great general, of the great statesman, of the great legislator' (*TMS* VI. i. 15).

I have said that the new part VI, 'Of the Character of Virtue', was inserted in the sixth edition to make good an omission. Yet it fails to do the most important part of the task required. To understand why, we need to look at the earlier version of the book.

We find there a theory built up by careful stages from a simple base. Part I explains judgements of propriety and impropriety (that is to say, simple judgements of right and wrong) made about the actions of other people. Part II explains the rather more complex judgements of merit and demerit, again as made about the actions of other people. Part III explains moral judgements made about one's own actions; it claims that these are more complex still, because they depend upon a knowledge of judgements about others. Part IV, focusing upon the concept of utility, shows the relevance of aesthetic judgement both to ethics and to economics. Part V continues broadening the perspective by examining the sociological background of aesthetic and moral judgement. That completes the theory. The final part of the book (VI in the first five editions, VII in the sixth edition) is a survey of the history of moral philosophy, classifying and criticizing the main types of theory with the aim of showing how Smith's own theory accounts for the element of truth in earlier theories while avoiding their weaknesses.

After an introductory paragraph, the final part of the book begins its serious business with a statement of the task of moral philosophy, the passage I have quoted in Chapter 1. It specifies two problems, the nature of virtue and the nature of moral judgement; but the preceding five parts of the book have focused on the second problem alone. There is an elaborate, systematic theory of moral judgement, and there are some incidental remarks about particular virtues, but nothing remotely resembling a systematic theory of the nature of virtue. In short, the book does not live up to the programme set for moral philosophy.

Smith himself may have realized the discrepancy when he came to revise the work for the fourth edition (1774), since the original title, 'The Theory of Moral Sentiments', was there supplemented by a subtitle (quoted in Chapter 1) which is a precise description of Smith's method of handling his main theme, moral judgement. I think that the new part VI, added to the sixth edition, is intended to repair the omission of a thorough treatment of the other main problem announced in the programme of the final part, but it seems unlikely that Smith had the task consistently in mind from 1774 onwards. The fifth edition (1781) contains no revisions of real substance. Smith wrote on 21 April 1785 to his publisher, Thomas Cadell, welcoming the information that a new edition of *The Wealth of Nations* was called for, and added: 'If a new edition of the theory [meaning *The Theory of Moral Sentiments*] is wanted I have a few alterations to make of no great consequence which I shall send to you.'[1] He then mentioned a projected new edition in a letter of 1 November 1785 to the Duc de La Rochefoucauld. This too does not suggest any extensive revision and says that Smith hoped to do the

---

[1] *Correspondence of Adam Smith*, 281; letter no. 244.

work 'before the end of the ensuing winter'.² On 14 March 1786 he asked Cadell what demand there still was for the book.³ Then on 15 March 1788, in another letter to Cadell, Smith wrote of 'giving the most intense application' to a revision of the *Moral Sentiments*, 'to all parts of which I am making many additions and corrections'. Even at that stage, however, he does not mention a new part VI. On the contrary, he says: 'The chief and the most important additions will be to the third part, that concerning *the sense of Duty* and to the last part concerning *the History of Moral Philosophy*.'⁴ The idea of adding the new part VI evidently came later. Smith refers to it in a further letter to Cadell dated 31 March 1789: 'Besides the Additions and improvements I mentioned to you; I have inserted, immediately after the fifth part, a compleat new sixth part containing a practical system of Morality, under the title of the Character of Virtue.'⁵

'A practical system of morality': that is a fair description of the new part VI. But what has happened to Smith's original requirement that a treatise of moral philosophy should explain the nature of virtue? The requirement did indeed include the content of virtue, which is what we are now given; but the essential problem was to find a theory that explains that content, just as the second problem assigned to moral philosophy was to find a theory that explains moral judgement.

In the old part VI (now part VII), Smith's statement of the two problems is immediately followed by a summary of three theories about the first problem and four theories about the second. On the first problem, Hutcheson had said that virtue consists in benevolence, Samuel Clarke had said 'acting suitably to the different relations we stand in', others had said a prudent pursuit of our own happiness (*TMS* VII. i. 3). The next section then spells out these three types of theory, but in a different order. The first chapter deals with 'those Systems which make Virtue consist in Propriety'. It begins with three theories from the ancient world, those of Plato, Aristotle, and the

² *Correspondence of Adam Smith*, 286; letter no. 248.
³ Ibid. 293; letter no. 257.
⁴ Ibid. 310–11; letter no. 276.   ⁵ Ibid. 320; letter no. 287.

Stoics. It then proceeds to the 'modern systems' of Samuel Clarke, his follower William Wollaston, and (oddly enough) the third Earl of Shaftesbury, who was in fact a thinker of a very different stamp. Smith bundles these strange bedfellows together because they all (as he thinks) say that an action is virtuous because its motive is proper or suitable to its object or to nature. The second chapter deals with 'systems' that make virtue consist in prudence, the prime example being that of Epicurus, and the third chapter is on the benevolence theory, with Hutcheson as the prime example.

Smith then says that all theories of virtue can be reduced to one or other of the three he has discussed. In the final paragraph of the third chapter, he says that Hume's theory (that qualities of the mind are virtuous if agreeable or useful) is a form of the propriety theory because it implies that 'virtue consists not in any one affection, but in the proper degree of all the affections' (*TMS* VII. ii. 3. 21). He then ends by saying that his own theory is in the same boat, the only difference being that Hume's theory 'makes utility, and not sympathy, or the correspondent affection of the spectator, the measure of this proper degree'. (The sixth edition says 'the natural and original measure'.)

And that, apparently, is Adam Smith's contribution to debate on 'the nature of virtue'. The correct theory, that virtue consists in propriety, is shared by Plato, Aristotle, the Stoics, Clarke, Wollaston, Shaftesbury, Hume, and Smith. The earlier forms of the theory are, however, inadequate in not specifying how propriety or suitability is measured; Smith remedies the defect with his theory of judgement based on sympathy.

As a solution of what is supposed to be one of the two main problems of moral philosophy, this is disappointingly thin, in stark contrast to Smith's ingenious and well-constructed solution of the second problem. As I have said in Chapter 1, Smith gives us a full and clear account of the content of virtue, that is, the cardinal virtues and the relation between them, but fails to provide an enlightening explanation of the concept itself, as he does with the topic of moral judgement. Such an explanation would show how the concept of moral virtue arises and how it distinguishes moral excellence from other forms of human excellence. The account we are given, that virtue consists in propriety, is too vague to be an explanation and too wide to differentiate it from the rival theories, for it is very easy to argue that a policy of prudence is pre-eminently acting conformably or suitably to nature, and it is not difficult to mount a similar argument for benevolence. This propriety theory of virtue also sits ill with distinctions drawn elsewhere between propriety and virtue. In part I Smith says there is 'a considerable difference between virtue and mere propriety', the former calling for admiration, the latter for simple approval (*TMS* I. i. 5. 7–8); and in part VII itself he says that propriety is a necessary condition of all virtue but not a sufficient condition of virtues such as beneficence that call for a 'superior degree of esteem' going beyond approval (*TMS* VII. ii. 1. 50). The plain fact is that Smith has not thought out an answer to the first problem set by his programme. When he came to write the new part VI he tried to repair the omission after a fashion but still did not come to grips with the original problem.

9

The Cardinal Virtues

It remains to say what is distinctive about Smith's view of the cardinal virtues. They are prudence, justice, beneficence, and self-command. Surprisingly they do not include courage, surprisingly because Smith himself greatly admired courage and knew well that it had a pre-eminent place among the virtues of the Greeks and Romans. The word 'courage' (or 'fortitude') crops up occasionally in the *Moral Sentiments*, but the only place where it has more than a chance mention is in Smith's historical account of the virtues in Plato, Aristotle, and Epicurus. His personal esteem of courage is manifest in the contempt that he expresses for Bishop Massillon's disparagement of military life as compared with the life of a monk (*TMS* III. 2. 34–5).

What is distinctive in his view of prudence? Since prudence is the rational pursuit of self-interest, you might expect the economist in Smith to associate prudence with enterprise; but in fact he plays this down: 'It [prudence] is rather cautious than enterprising, and more anxious to preserve the advantages which we already possess, than forward to prompt us to the acquisition of still greater advantages' (*TMS* VI. i. 6). Caution is the watchword of the discussion, sensibly enough for a moral philosopher's analysis of prudence as commonly understood. It is noteworthy that Smith, after having written his great work on economics, could revert so wholeheartedly in 1789 to the pure role of the moral philosopher. The modest place that he assigns to prudence, as ordinarily understood, goes along with his judgement that it rates only a 'cold esteem', being 'regarded as a most respectable and even, in some degree, as an amiable and agreeable quality, yet it never is considered as one of the most endearing, or of the most ennobling of the virtues' (*TMS* VI. i. 14).

He contrasts it with the 'superior prudence' that has nothing to do with self-interest, 'the prudence of the great general, of the great statesman, of the great legislator'. This is always combined with greater virtues, valour, benevolence, justice, self-command, and appears to be the icing of wisdom on the cake of other virtues. 'It is the best head joined to the best heart. It is the most perfect wisdom combined with the most perfect virtue' (*TMS* VI. i. 15).

I turn next to justice. Smith's thoughts on justice are mainly given in part II of the *Moral Sentiments*, that is, in the original version of the book. The general subject of part II is merit and demerit. Its first section deals with the sense of merit and demerit, and then the second section is entitled 'Of Justice and Beneficence'. That section in fact says little about beneficence but quite a lot about justice, and this affords a reason why the new part VI, added in 1789 to remedy a defect, deals extensively with beneficence and only briefly with justice. (I have suggested an additional reason in the preceding chapter.)

The discussion of justice in part II, section ii, is concerned with justice in relation to merit or desert. Beneficent actions deserve reward and deliberately harmful actions deserve punishment. The propriety of reward and punishment consists in the approval by spectators of the natural reaction of those affected, gratitude for being benefited, and resentment for being harmed. Justice differs from other virtues in that it is attended by a greater degree of obligation to conform; consequently a breach of justice renders the offender liable to the enforced imposition of the punishment it deserves. Smith is thinking of criminal justice and says nothing at this point about the notion of equity or fairness as a prime element in the concept of justice.

He does, however, refer to fairness en passant when he writes of the resentment aroused by 'injury', a breach of justice. Impartial spectators will 'indulge' a man's self-interested effort to outdo competitors in 'the race' for wealth or honour, but if he should stoop to some unfair step comparable to jostling or throwing down a rival in a race, their indulgence will end.

It is a violation of fair play, which they cannot admit of. This man is to them, in every respect, as good as he: they do not enter into that self-love by which he prefers himself so much to this other, and cannot go along with the motive from which he hurt him. They readily, therefore, sympathize with the natural resentment of the injured, and the offender becomes the object of their hatred and indignation. (*TMS* II. ii. 2.1)

Self-interest is a primeval motive and the dominant tendency in human nature; a sense of fairness and the limitation of self-interest come from the stance of a spectator. This sense of fairness includes a notion of equality as between one person and another.

When Smith writes more briefly of justice in the final part of the book, he distinguishes three senses of the term. He calls the first commutative justice and says that this is what he has discussed in part II as a principle that may be enforced by punishment. He now describes it as abstaining from harm to others in person, estate, or reputation. The second and third senses are simply uses of the term 'just' in a wide sense. One is 'proper beneficence', benefiting other people in accordance with merit or as generosity prompts. The other is valuing or pursuing something, for others or for oneself, with the degree of esteem that the impartial spectator would think it deserved; Smith illustrates this usage with the expression 'failing to do justice' to something or to oneself. Smith's explanation of these two senses of justice includes, in both cases, a reference to merit or desert, thus retaining a connection with his basic idea of the concept of justice; but he himself acknowledges that these senses are not specific. He says that the second sense of justice 'comprehends all the social virtues' and that the third (exemplified in Plato's *Republic*) means the same as perfect propriety and covers virtue of all kinds (*TMS* VII. ii. 1. 10).

Smith clearly regards the 'commutative' sense as the main one. It is a negative principle, abstaining from harm to others, and this seems remote from present-day ideas of justice. We would of course think it a basic principle of right action but we would not associate it specifically with justice. Philosophical discussion of justice nowadays tends to be focused upon distributive justice and its criteria of merit, equality, and need. In Adam Smith's day the relief of need was assigned to charity or benevolence, not justice, though there is a whisper in Thomas Reid of a possible connection between need and justice.[1] A firm move in that direction had to wait for the nineteenth century.

The more extensive discussion of beneficence in part VI is worked out under a distinctive analysis, dealing first with beneficence towards individuals, then with beneficence towards 'societies', and finally with the ideal of universal benevolence. In all three categories Smith is thinking of what is 'recommended by nature', the natural inclination to benefit certain groups of other people; and he takes it for granted that this natural inclination is also a moral obligation.

Beneficence towards individuals is directed most strongly upon one's family and gives precedence to children over parents. This is rational as well as natural, Smith says, for the continued existence of a child depends upon the care of its parents, while the converse does not hold. 'In the eye of nature, it would seem, a child is a more important object than an old man; and excites a much more lively, as well as a much more universal sympathy.' Rightly so, for this accords with their potentialities. 'Every thing may be expected, or at least hoped, from the child. In ordinary cases, very little can be either expected or hoped from the old man' (*TMS* vi. ii. 1. 3). Next in line, at least in early 'friendship', are brothers and sisters, followed by cousins, and then by the children of cousins.

This recital of the obvious leads to a non-obvious connection with Smith's characteristic psychology: 'What is called affection, is in reality nothing but habitual sympathy.' More precisely, it is either the actual feeling of habitual sympathy or the 'necessary consequences'

---

[1] Thomas Reid, *Essays on the Active Powers of Man* (1788), essay 5, ch. 5; repr. in vol. iii of *Essays on the Powers of the Human Mind* (Edinburgh: Bell & Bradfute; London: Longman, etc., 1808), 432.

of such feeling. By 'necessary consequences' Smith seems to mean expected and obligatory consequences. People do usually feel an habitual sympathy with those individuals with whom they regularly consort. It is therefore expected and taken to be the norm. We are shocked when we find, on occasion, that it does not happen. It seems 'the highest impropriety, and sometimes even a sort of impiety' (*TMS* vi. ii. 1. 7).

There are circumstances, however, Smith continues, in which the normal frequency of meetings between relatives does not take place. For example, a child may be separated in infancy from its father and then come back when adult; or siblings may happen to be educated in different countries. This inevitably diminishes the natural feeling of affection that is the norm. Yet respect for the general rule remains and produces a semblance of the normal feeling. 'When they meet, it is often with so strong a disposition to conceive that habitual sympathy which constitutes the family affection, that they are very apt to fancy that they have actually conceived it' (*TMS* vi. ii. 1. 8).

All this seems at first sight a piece of acute psychological observation such as we often find in Adam Smith. But it is not wholly sound and shows that Smith, like most philosophers, can at times make facts fit his theory instead of making theory fit facts. His view that affection between members of a family is really habitual sympathy can apply well enough to the affection of children towards parents and of siblings towards each other, but not to the affection of parents towards their children. Habitual sympathy may reinforce but cannot constitute the initial affection that most parents feel for their children. It is particularly striking in mothers, less so in fathers, though still apparent to some degree. Certainly mothers commonly feel right away a strong sense of love for the child they have borne. No doubt it is connected with the pain of giving birth and the long discomfort of gestation, a feeling perhaps of very special and well-deserved ownership. It clearly is not, and does not depend upon, sympathy with the feelings of the child, if indeed one can properly speak of feelings in a newly born baby. To be sure, the mother, and the father too, are strongly motivated to care for the child; they are aware that the child has needs and they feel obliged to meet those needs. But it is bizarre to suppose that this feeling of obligation, or the feeling of affection, rests upon thought of a correspondence between the inferred experience of the child and an imagined hypothetical experience of the parent if in the place of the child.

The motivation to care for the child is, of course, partly innate, instinctive, a tendency shared with other animals. That, however, is not relevant to the question whether Smith's observation is sound. Smith would not say that his observation applies to non-human animals with consciousness. Some animal consciousness may include feeling, but it would be foolhardy to suppose that such feeling is comparable with human sympathy and its associate, imagination.

Smith's chapter on beneficence towards 'societies' is mainly concerned with the state. He does briefly mention lesser societies within the state and says, unsurprisingly, that they are and should be treated as subordinate to the state since they are dependent on it for their security and protection. As regards the state itself, Smith says that the love of one's country involves two principles, respect for the established constitution and the desire to promote the welfare of fellow-citizens. In normal times of peace the two principles go together, but in times of turbulence such as war or civil faction they may draw apart. On that point Smith writes at some length about a revolutionary 'spirit of system' that invades the normal benevolent 'public spirit' and produces disorder. He may be echoing d'Alembert's use of the phrase 'spirit of system' (in the Preliminary Discourse of the French *Encyclopédie*) when criticizing philosophical rationalists, and he may also have in mind the French Revolution (part VI was written in 1789). In general, however, Smith's account of beneficence towards societies has no special significance for his ethical theory.

The title of the next chapter is 'Of universal Benevolence', as contrasted with the word 'Beneficence' in the preceding one. The first sentence emphasizes the point of the change: 'Though our good offices can very seldom be extended to any wider society than that of our own country; our good-will is circumscribed by no boundary, but may embrace the immensity of the universe' (*TMS* VI. ii. 3. 1). This short chapter, unlike most of Smith's writing, is openly prescriptive: he normally uses the descriptive language of sociological observation. In this chapter he says that the wise and virtuous man 'should' be willing to see all other interests sacrificed to 'the greater interest of the universe'; that, in great public disasters, he 'ought' to consider that he has been ordered to help; that he 'should' be capable of acting as a good soldier would.

Such idealistic thought, in Smith's view, must go along with theological belief. Universal benevolence cannot bring 'solid happiness' to anyone unless he believes that the universe is governed by a benevolent God who directs it 'so as at all times to produce the greatest possible quantity of happiness' (*TMS* VI. ii. 3. 5). This is the chapter from which Professor John Dunn culled the quotation, 'the very suspicion of a fatherless world, must be the most melancholy of all reflections'. Dunn, supposing it to have been published in 1759, used it to illustrate Adam Smith's religious belief in his youth as against the 'practical atheism' of his old age. Since it was in fact written for the sixth edition of 1790, one must instead regard it as firm evidence that Smith never was a practical atheist, although there is evidence elsewhere in the book that he did abandon his early adherence to Christian doctrine.[2]

Last but not least in Smith's group of cardinal virtues is self-command. Self-command is one of the cardinal virtues in Plato's *Republic*, where it appears under the name of *sophrosyne*, commonly translated as temperance or restraint. A distinctive feature of Smith's account is the influence of self-command on all passions in moderating any tendency to excess. Some passions, notably fear and anger, are especially liable to boil up to an inordinate degree and are difficult to restrain. Others, usually of a selfish character such as the love of ease, pleasure, or applause, can be restrained for the moment without great effort but are persistent in recurring and so call for

---

[2] I discussed this evidence in 'Adam Smith and "the infection of David Hume's society"'. See Ch. 5 n. 1.

constant vigilance. Smith attributes a special merit to self-command because it involves deliberate and often difficult restraint, unlike the normal exercise of the other cardinal virtues. It can also help those other virtues to prevail when they have to contend with temptation. It has therefore 'the character of the most exalted wisdom and virtue. Self-command is not only itself a great virtue, but from it all the other virtues seem to derive their principal lustre' (*TMS* vi. iii. 11).

10

Virtue and Beauty

Many of the British moralists of the seventeenth and eighteenth centuries comment on the relation between virtue and beauty. Hobbes has a simple view, easy to understand though not easy to accept. He defines good as the object of desire, and evil as the object of aversion. He then says that words for the beautiful and the ugly come close to those for good and evil but are not precisely the same: *pulchrum* (or an English equivalent) means that which promises good, while *turpe* means that which promises evil.[1]

Lord Shaftesbury's account is far from simple. He compares beauty with virtue and distinguishes both of them from 'mere goodness' because the sense of virtue and that of beauty share the special factor of being objects of 'reflection'. He explains the difference as follows.

A judgement of good or ill is the result of 'affection' (feeling). When such a judgement is applied to a person or other sensible creature, it indicates that the said creature contributes to the well-being or ill-being of the system of which it forms a part. The idea of virtue can apply only to human beings and is directed upon actions or feelings that are 'brought into the mind by reflection'. Shaftesbury uses this phrase to distinguish objects of sense-perception (including internal sensation) from objects that we get to know by thought ('reflection') about the objects of sense-perception. When we think about (reflect upon) feelings that can be judged good or bad, we experience second-order feelings about those initial feelings. Favourable second-order feelings are given expression in the idea of

---

[1] Hobbes, *Leviathan*, I. 6; Raphael (ed.), *British Moralists*, §25.

moral virtue or worthiness, while unfavourable second-order feelings are expressed in the idea of vice or unworthiness.

Similar second-order feelings arise when we contemplate the 'arrangement and disposition' of the 'shapes, motions, colours, and proportions' of the objects of perception. We are affected favourably or unfavourably, feeling 'the soft and harsh, the agreeable and disagreeable', and we express those feelings by judgements of 'fair and foul', 'harmonious and dissonant'. This constitutes our sense of the sublime and beautiful.[2]

The complicated analysis that I have outlined is given in Shaftesbury's *Inquiry concerning Virtue, or Merit*. In a later work, *The Moralists*, there is a more succinct and more popular version of Shaftesbury's views on the relation between beauty and virtue. He says there that disagreement on the relative degree of beauty or of virtue in particular instances does not prevent universal agreement on the genuine existence of beauty and of moral goodness, and that the two participants discussing beauty and virtue in this work are ready to relate them, finding fit and decent actions to be handsome, so much so that they have 'decreed that *beauty and good are still the same*'.[3]

Francis Hutcheson carried much further the analogy between beauty and virtue. The other authors, generally speaking, focus chiefly on the nature of virtue itself and regard its relation to beauty as a subordinate topic. Hutcheson, however, in his first book, *An Inquiry into the Original of our Ideas of Beauty and Virtue*, is as much interested in aesthetics as in ethics. The work contains two treatises, each a full-scale discussion of its subject. They share the common aim of refuting the notion, ascribed to Hobbes and Bernard Mandeville, that all favourable feelings and motives must be self-interested, and

---

[2] Shaftesbury, *An Inquiry concerning Virtue, or Merit*, I. ii. 3; Raphael (ed.), *British Moralists*, §201.

[3] Shaftesbury, *The Moralists, a philosophical rhapsody* (1709), III. ii; included in *Characteristics of Men, Manners, Opinions, and Times* (1711), ed. Lawrence E. Klein (Cambridge: Cambridge University Press, 1999), 327; or Selby-Bigge, *British Moralists*, i. 66.

they explicitly acknowledge that they are following in the steps of Shaftesbury.

In the second of these treatises, *An Inquiry concerning Moral Good and Evil*, Hutcheson frequently writes of moral approval as equivalent to finding beauty in its object. He sums up the position of empiricist writers on ethics in his introduction: they hold 'that we are determined to perceive some *beauty*' in the actions that we call virtuous. The notion is repeated at several points elsewhere: God has 'made virtue a lovely form'; virtue is 'the beauty of action'; we have 'a distinct perception of *beauty* or *excellence* in kind affections'; the moral sense 'makes benevolent actions appear beautiful'; virtue is 'called *amiable* or *lovely*'; useful actions that do not proceed from benevolent intention are 'void of moral beauty'; different types of benevolence have 'different degrees of moral beauty'; 'we have a *sense* of *goodness* and *moral beauty*' in virtuous actions; virtue has a 'powerful charm above all other kinds of *beauty*'.[4]

The affinity between virtue and beauty leads him to speak of a moral sense comparable with the common conception of a sense of beauty. He does not think that his use of the word 'sense' is metaphorical, although he recognizes that the sense of beauty and the moral sense do not have any connection with a bodily organ, as do the senses of sight, touch, taste, smell, and hearing. He calls them internal senses, following John Locke's suggestion of 'internal sense' as a name for introspection.

John Balguy, a rationalist critic of Hutcheson, shows a pleasingly open mind on the relation between virtue and beauty. He has no doubt that Hutcheson is mistaken in founding the perception of virtue and the motivation to it upon feeling alone. He agrees, of course, that feeling does play a part but he thinks its role is subsidiary to that of rational understanding. He then examines the aesthetic aspect of virtue, since virtue, he thinks, may be considered under

---

[4] The quotations from Francis Hutcheson, *An Inquiry into the Original of our Ideas of Beauty and Virtue* (rev. 4th edn., 1738), may be found in *Francis Hutcheson: Philosophical Writings*, ed. R. S. Downie (London: Dent, 1994), 69, 5, 44, 70, 72, 76, 86, 88, 95, 104; or (most of them) in Raphael (ed.), *British Moralists*, §§305, 307, 314, 328, 331, 340.

the notion of *pulchrum* as well as *honestum*: 'As to the *pulchrum* or *beauty* of virtue, it seems to me somewhat doubtful and difficult to determine, whether the *understanding* alone be sufficient for the perception of it.' One would suppose, he says, that the beauty of virtue is a necessary attachment, but in practice we find that, while there is, normally, general agreement among rational people on what is right and just, this is not true of their perception of the beauty of such actions: some people do not see beauty in all virtuous actions, and all people find some virtuous actions more beautiful than others although equally right.

That was what he wrote in the original version of his tract *The Foundation of Moral Goodness*, published in 1728. But by 1734 he had changed his mind and added a note to say that he had now 'been convinced, that all beauty, whether moral or natural, is to be reckoned and reputed as a species of absolute truth' perceived by the understanding. In other words, he had decided not to qualify his rationalism on the perception of values.[5]

David Hume is more emphatic than Hutcheson in comparing virtue with beauty, and more explicit in locating a common source, sympathy.

To have the sense of virtue, is nothing but to *feel* a satisfaction of a particular kind from the contemplation of a character. The very *feeling* constitutes our praise or admiration.... The case is the same as in our judgements concerning all kinds of beauty, and tastes, and sensations. Our approbation is implied in the immediate pleasure they convey to us.[6]

Our sense of beauty depends very much on this principle [of sympathy]; and where any object has a tendency to produce pleasure in its possessor, it is always regarded as beautiful... Wherever an object has a tendency to produce pleasure in the possessor... it is sure to please the spectator, by a delicate sympathy with the possessor. . . .

    [5] John Balguy, *The Foundation of Moral Goodness*, I. 5; Raphael (ed.), *British Moralists*, §443 and n.
    [6] Hume, *A Treatise of Human Nature*, III. i. 2; Raphael (ed.), *British Moralists*, §506.

The same principle produces, in many instances, our sentiments of morals, as well as those of beauty. . . . Now as . . . the good of society, where our own interest is not concerned, or that of our friends, pleases only by sympathy: it follows, that sympathy is the source of the esteem, which we pay to all the artificial virtues. . . . From thence we may presume, that it also gives rise to many of the other virtues.[7]

These quotations come from Hume's first, and major, work, *A Treatise of Human Nature*, published in 1739–40. A later work, *An Enquiry concerning the Principles of Morals*, published in 1751, goes a little further, projecting moral approval onto its object so as to speak of 'moral beauty' comparable with 'natural beauty'.

This doctrine [that moral judgement rests on sentiment] will become still more evident, if we compare moral beauty with natural, to which, in many particulars, it bears so near a resemblance. . . . Euclid has fully explained all the qualities of the circle; but has not, in any proposition, said a word of its beauty. The reason is evident. The beauty is not a quality of the circle. . . . It is only the effect, which that figure produces upon the mind, whose peculiar fabric or structure renders it susceptible of such sentiments. . . . Again, attend to Cicero, while he paints the crimes of a Verres or a Catiline; you must acknowledge that the moral turpitude results, in the same manner, from the contemplation of the whole, when presented to a being, whose organs have such a particular structure and formation.[8]

Henry Home, Lord Kames (he acquired the title as a Scottish judge), wrote extensively on jurisprudence, moral philosophy, and aesthetics. He is more sure-footed in aesthetics than in ethics and it is not surprising that he should relate the two. What *is* surprising is that he regards aesthetic judgement as more basic than ethical. He does so because the scope of aesthetic judgement is wider. The fundamental reaction to human experience, according to Kames, is a feeling of pleasure or pain, and this is well-nigh universal in its scope. 'As we are placed in a great world, surrounded with beings

[7] Hume, *Treatise*, III. iii. 1; Raphael (ed.), *British Moralists*, §§547–9.
[8] Hume, *An Enquiry concerning the Principles of Morals*, app. I; Raphael (ed.), *British Moralists*, §§603–4.

and things, some beneficial, some hurtful; we are so constituted, that scarce any object is indifferent to us. It either gives pleasure or pain.'[9] This is most notable with the objects of sight: we call 'beautiful' those that give us pleasure, and 'ugly' those that give pain. Then we apply the same words metaphorically to almost anything that gives pleasure or pain, and this usage has become so common that it is hardly considered metaphorical.

Kames then distinguishes three levels of beauty and ugliness. The lowest applies to objects whose existence is not thought of as related to an end or a purposive agent; he gives the example of a flowing river. The second level concerns objects that *are* so related, such as works of art or other products of human effort. Our appreciation of their beauty or ugliness includes approbation or disapprobation. Approbation in this sense does not imply approbation of the end served; it simply indicates the pleasure of perceiving that the object succeeds in serving a purpose. If we do approve of the end served, then our appreciation is of the highest form of beauty, the third level; conversely, if we disapprove of the end served we are experiencing the highest form of ugliness.

When we take the end itself under consideration, there is discovered a beauty or ugliness of a higher kind than the two former. A beneficial end proposed, strikes us with a very peculiar pleasure: and approbation belongs also to this feeling. Thus, the mechanism of a ship is beautiful, in the view of means well fitted to an end. But the end itself, of carrying on commerce, and procuring so many conveniencies to mankind, exalts the object, and heightens our approbation and pleasure.[10]

Kames notes that his analysis allows for permutations at the third stage: we might think an object well fitted to serve a bad end, or ill fitted to serve a good end. However, the important conclusion is that the third stage of beauty and deformity may be applied to thought about human actions; there the factor of deliberate intention gives

⁹ Henry Home, Lord Kames, *Essays on the Principles of Morality and Natural Religion* (1751), II. ii; quoted from Selby-Bigge, *British Moralists*, ii. 302.
¹⁰ Kames, *Essays*, II. ii; Selby-Bigge, *British Moralists*, ii. 303–4.

rise to a special form of beauty and deformity, as anyone may see if he attends carefully to what goes on in his mind.

Let him but attend to a deliberate action, suggested by filial piety, or suggested by gratitude; such action will not only be agreeable to him, and appear beautiful, but will be agreeable and beautiful, as fit, right, and meet to be done.... This distinguishing circumstance intitles the beauty and deformity of human actions to peculiar names: they are termed moral beauty and moral deformity. Hence the morality and immorality of human actions; and the power or faculty by which we perceive this difference among actions, passeth under the name of the moral sense.[11]

Richard Price, a rationalist philosopher who thinks and writes with enviable clarity, draws a firm distinction between moral and aesthetic judgement. He discusses beauty only because Hutcheson and Hume couple it with virtue. In criticizing them Price makes shrewd use of language. His book, *A Review of the Principal Questions in Morals*, concentrates firmly on ethics, and the chapter that discusses beauty states in its title that it is about the notion of the beauty and deformity 'of actions'. While the first sentence makes the more general statement that he is going to discuss 'our ideas of *beauty*, and its contrary', the paragraph that follows gives the nub of his argument in terms of common statements about actions—that they are not only right or wrong but also 'amiable' or 'odious and shocking'. He assumes ready acceptance that these terms are virtual synonyms of 'beautiful' and 'ugly', and of course they carry on their face a reference to the feelings of spectators. Price is granting that value judgements about actions do often include an aesthetic element but insists that this is an accompaniment, not the essence, of their reference to virtue or vice. He supports his case by noting that the aesthetic addition to such judgements is confined to actions of high moral worth.

But it may be farther worth observing, that the epithets *beautiful* and *amiable* are, in common language, confined to actions and characters

---

[11] Kames, *Essays*, II. ii; Selby-Bigge, *British Moralists*, ii. 305.

that please us *highly*, from the peculiar degree of moral worth and virtue apprehended in them. All virtuous actions must be pleasing to an intelligent observer; but they do not all please to the degree necessary to entitle them to these epithets, as we generally apply them.[12]

Adam Smith will have been aware of some, though not all, of these comparisons between virtue and beauty. He was familiar with the work of Hobbes and Shaftesbury, to both of whom he refers explicitly; and of course he knew well the writings of his teacher Hutcheson, his close friend Hume, and his patron Kames, who had helped to arrange for him to give public lectures in Edinburgh and had supported his initial academic appointment at Glasgow. Smith appears not to have known of Richard Price's book on moral philosophy, which was first published a year after the first edition of the *Moral Sentiments*, but he might have had his attention drawn to Price's generous reference to his work in the appendix to the third edition of the *Review of Morals* (1787).[13]

Smith's own discussions of the subject show that he thought it important. He claims originality for one element of his contribution and evidently took pride in it. The relevant passage is in part IV of the *Moral Sentiments*, announced as dealing with the effect of utility on the sentiment of approbation. This effect is described as adding 'beauty' to human productions and to human action and character.

Smith begins by paying tribute to Hume for explaining why the awareness of utility gives pleasure, namely because it reminds us of the pleasure or convenience of the end that it serves. He then adds that no one has explained a curious further fact, that we often value the utility of the means more than we value the end, even though the end is what gives point to the means. For example, a person who is keen on watches despises a watch that loses two or three minutes a day, so he sells it for a couple of guineas and buys for fifty guineas a more reliable watch that loses no more than a minute in a fortnight.

---

[12] Richard Price, *A Review of the Principal Questions in Morals* (rev. 3rd edn., 1787), ch. 2; ed. D. D. Raphael (Oxford: Clarendon Press, 1948; corrected repr., 1974), 64.

[13] Ibid., app. n. D, 281–2.

His concern is not so much to have an accurate knowledge of the time, but rather to have a near-perfect machine for telling the time. The tendency is, however, not confined to such trivial examples: 'it is often the secret motive of the most serious and important pursuits of both private and public life' (*TMS* IV. 1. 7). We now learn why Smith attaches such importance to his novel 'principle'. His account is in unusually vivid language.

The poor man's son, whom heaven in its anger has visited with ambition . . . admires the condition of the rich. He finds the cottage of his father too small for his accommodation, and fancies he should be lodged more at his ease in a palace. . . . He is enchanted with the distant idea of this felicity . . . and . . . he devotes himself for ever to the pursuit of wealth and greatness. To obtain the conveniencies which these afford, he submits in the first year, nay in the first month of his application, to more fatigue of body and more uneasiness of mind than he could have suffered through the whole of his life from the want of them. . . . in the last dregs of life . . . he begins at last to find that wealth and greatness are mere trinkets of frivolous utility. . . . Power and riches appear then to be, what they are, enormous and operose machines contrived to produce a few trifling conveniencies . . . which must be kept in order with the most anxious attention. (*TMS* IV. 1. 8)

Is this what Smith himself thinks to be true of wealth and greatness? It seems so, since he says here that power and riches *are* what they then appear to be. Yet in the next paragraph he describes this account as a 'splenetic philosophy' which 'in time of sickness or low spirits . . . entirely depreciates those great objects of human desire'. We take a different view in better health or spirits: 'we are then charmed with the beauty of that accommodation which reigns in the palaces and oeconomy of the great.' This, however, is not the last word. Smith immediately goes back to the view that, if we consider 'the real satisfaction' of the life of the rich and the great, 'it will always appear in the highest degree contemptible and trifling'. The rosier view, which comes more naturally, is the result of confusing the reality with the beauty of the system, that is, 'the order, the regular and harmonious movement of the system, the machine or oeconomy by means of which it is produced' (*TMS* IV. 1. 9).

Smith then says: 'And it is well that nature imposes upon us in this manner. It is this deception which rouses and keeps in continual motion the industry of mankind.' The paragraph proceeds to enlarge upon the benefits of this 'deception', and includes one of Smith's famous references to the invisible hand that produces unintended consequences. The invisible hand in this context leads the rich to share the necessities of life with the poor.

(In *The Wealth of Nations* the invisible hand leads 'every individual' to promote the public interest without intending it. The unintended consequence there is the production of maximum public happiness, while in the *Moral Sentiments* passage the unintended consequence is the distribution of means to happiness. There is an even earlier use of the image in Smith's essay on Astronomy, where the invisible hand is held to be responsible for irregular events in nature.)

So it seems that the benefits of social life, amply set out in Smith's great work on economics, rest upon a deception. And, although the paragraph begins by saying that the deception is imposed by 'nature', it speaks later of 'Providence' as responsible and as not having forgotten or abandoned the poor, who are not really inferior in 'the real happiness of human life'. The paragraph ends with the astonishing statement: 'In ease of body and peace of mind, all the different ranks of life are nearly upon a level, and the beggar who suns himself by the side of the highway, possesses that security which kings are fighting for' (*TMS* IV. 1. 10).

Can Smith have really believed that? The passage was written for the first edition of 1759, when the young professor in his thirties may well have entertained some romantic notions and thought them suitable for students mostly destined for the ministry. Yet he left it unaltered when he revised the book in 1789, long after he had written *The Wealth of Nations*. Perhaps he thought it too fine a flourish to be lost, or perhaps he remained genuinely ambivalent.

Smith's discussions of virtue in relation to beauty are often marked by a special interest in drama when drawing on examples of finding ethics in the arts. He refers to Sophocles' *Philoctetes* and *Trachiniae*, Euripides' *Hippolytus*, Thomas Otway's *The Orphan*, Racine's *Phèdre*,

Shakespeare's *Othello* and *Hamlet*, Thomas Southerne's *The Fatal Marriage*, and Voltaire's *Mahomet* and *L'Orphelin de la Chine*, as well as making some general comments on tragic drama in several places, sometimes coupling it with 'romance'.

To what extent could Smith have seen actual theatrical performances? Apart from the mention of *Hamlet*, which comes in the new part VI of the sixth edition of the *Moral Sentiments*, all the above references were in the first edition of 1759, when Smith was teaching at Glasgow. Could Smith, at that time, have seen actual theatrical performances? We know that he enjoyed opera during his stay in Paris in 1766, and he may well have attended the staging of plays too. But what could he have seen in Scotland by 1759? There was no theatre in Glasgow at that time; indeed in 1762, strangely enough, Smith served on a university committee that successfully opposed the establishment of a theatre in the city. Presumably there was also no theatre in Oxford, where Smith was a student from 1740 to 1746, for the anti-theatre petition of the Glasgow university committee in 1762 cited the example of Oxford in its support.[14] There was a theatre of sorts, eking out a tenuous existence, in Edinburgh during Smith's sojourn there from 1748 to 1751, and he may have attended some of its performances.[15]

Perhaps a more promising possibility lies in do-it-yourself exercises at his school. John Rae tells us, in his *Life of Adam Smith*, that acting in plays was a common pursuit in Scottish schools at that time.[16] The practice was opposed by the religious authorities, but the town councils, which ran the schools, refused to be told by presbyteries what they should or should not do. At the Burgh School of Kirkcaldy, where Adam Smith had his early education, the classics teacher was especially keen on drama. He wrote a play himself and got his pupils to present it in 1734. There is no evidence that Smith was one of the actors, but he would certainly have seen the performance and

[14] Ian Simpson Ross, *The Life of Adam Smith* (Oxford: Clarendon Press, 1995), 148.

[15] David Daiches, *Edinburgh* (London: Hamish Hamilton, 1978), 111, 165–8.

[16] John Rae, *Life of Adam Smith* (London: Macmillan, 1895; repr. New York: Kelley, 1965), 5–6.

may have seen others. So he would have known that attending the performance of a play is far better than just reading it. When we add that to the abundant evidence of the *Moral Sentiments* that he found drama a rich source of ethical reflection, we are bound to be puzzled by his opposition to the project for a theatre in Glasgow. It no doubt says something for his innate aesthetic appreciation, but nothing for his enlightenment—or courage.

Another characteristic feature of Smith's thought about virtue and beauty is his belief that ethical and aesthetic judgement both use two standards of evaluation, one ideal, the other more practical. This notion is introduced in the very first section of the *Moral Sentiments*. Smith writes of two standards of propriety that are used when we attribute praise or blame to actions. One is perfect propriety, an ideal that cannot be attained in practice, so that a reference to it makes all human actions 'blameable and imperfect'. The second standard is the level commonly attained: actions that surpass this are praised and those that fall below it are blamed. Smith then goes on to say that judgement of the arts follows the same pattern.

It is in the same manner that we judge of the productions of all the arts which address themselves to the imagination. When a critic examines the work of any of the great masters in poetry or painting, he may sometimes examine it by an idea of perfection, in his own mind, which neither that nor any other human work will ever come up to; and as long as he compares it with this standard, he can see nothing in it but faults and imperfections. But when he comes to consider the rank which it ought to hold among other works of the same kind, he necessarily compares it with a very different standard, the common degree of excellence which is usually attained in this particular art; and when he judges of it by this new measure, it may often appear to deserve the highest applause. (*TMS* I. i. 5. 10)

The notion of two standards of comparison is elaborated in the new part VI added to the sixth edition. Here, too, Smith has in mind an analogy with beauty and art. The discussion is much longer than the earlier account in part I. It is also taken more seriously, in that the first standard, perfect propriety, is not treated as altogether impractical. According to Smith, the wise and virtuous man gives his 'principal attention' to the first standard. 'He has studied this idea more than other people ... and is much more deeply enamoured of its exquisite and divine beauty.' He does his best 'to assimilate his own character to this archetype of perfection'. But he can have only a limited success, for 'he imitates the work of a divine artist, which can never be equalled'. He knows that he does get beyond the second standard of propriety exemplified in the conduct of most people, but he does not take any pride in that; since his model for himself is the first standard, he feels humbled and is 'stamped with the character of real modesty' (*TMS* VI. iii. 25).

The experience of 'the wise and virtuous man' is also the experience of 'the great artist', who 'feels always the real imperfection of his own best works, and is more sensible than any man how much they fall short of that ideal perfection of which he has formed some conception, which he imitates as well as he can, but which he despairs of ever equalling' (*TMS* VI. iii. 26).

In part V of the *Moral Sentiments* Smith writes of the influence of custom and fashion upon moral judgement. His observations reflect the variety of practice in different places and at different periods of time. He takes it for granted that he should preface his survey about moral judgement with one about aesthetic sensibility. He takes this for granted, because he treats moral judgement as a form of aesthetic appraisal: 'Since our sentiments concerning beauty of every kind, are so much influenced by custom and fashion, it cannot be expected, that those, concerning the beauty of conduct, should be entirely exempted from the dominion of those principles' (*TMS* V. 2. 1). He finds that there is a significant difference. Custom and fashion can cause any external object to be accepted as at least 'agreeable', but this is not true when it comes to judging character and conduct: the brutality of a Nero will always be feared and hated; the imbecility attributed to Nero's predecessor Claudius will always be ridiculed. So, while following Hutcheson and Hume in allying ethics with aesthetics, Adam Smith departs from them in perceiving that the alliance has its limits.

11

Ethics and Theology

Adam Smith does not regard ethics as dependent on theology and so there was no need for him to include any discussion of theology in his book on the theory of ethics. The book arose out of his lectures as Professor of Moral Philosophy at Glasgow, and those lectures, in accordance with the Scottish tradition at that time, covered natural theology, ethics, and jurisprudence, the last of these understood as theory of politics and economics as well as of law. After a few years in the post Smith worked up the ethics part of the course into his first book, *The Theory of Moral Sentiments*, the last paragraph of which expressed Smith's hope of producing 'another discourse' on 'the general principles of law and government' together with the history of changes that had taken place 'not only in what concerns justice, but in what concerns police, revenue, and arms, and whatever else is the object of law' (*TMS* VII. iv. 37). In his *Lectures on Jurisprudence* Smith explains the term 'police' as a French word, derived from the Greek *politeia*, meaning the policy of civil government, notably in regard to 'cleanliness, security, and cheapness or plenty'.[1]

Much later in his life Smith published *The Wealth of Nations*, which is of course primarily a systematic treatment of economics but also contains wide-ranging historical reflections. In the preface (entitled 'Advertisement') to the sixth edition of the *Moral Sentiments* Smith quotes the 'promise', in the last paragraph of the first edition, to write another book and says:

[1] Adam Smith, *Lectures on Jurisprudence*, ed. R. L. Meek, D. D. Raphael, and P. G. Stein (Oxford: Clarendon Press, 1978), LJ(B) §203.

In the *Enquiry concerning the Nature and Causes of the Wealth of Nations*, I have partly executed this promise; at least so far as concerns police, revenue, and arms. What remains, the theory of jurisprudence, which I have long projected, I have hitherto been hindered from executing. . . . Though my very advanced age leaves me . . . very little expectation of ever being able to execute this great work to my own satisfaction; yet, as I have not altogether abandoned the design . . . I have allowed the paragraph to remain as it was published more than thirty years ago.

Smith doubts his ability to produce the work to his own satisfaction, but that does not mean he had done nothing. In a letter of 1 November 1785 to the Duc de La Rochefoucauld, Smith says that, apart from revising the *Moral Sentiments*, he has 'two other great works on the anvil', a 'philosophical history' of literature and philosophy, and 'a sort of theory and History of Law and Government', for both of which he had collected most of 'the materials' and had put part of them 'into tollerable good order'.[2] When he was facing death in July 1790, he insisted that his friends Joseph Black and James Hutton should destroy most of his manuscripts, of which there had been, even in 1773, about eighteen volumes of thin paper.[3] We may be pretty sure that some of those volumes contained a draft of at least part of the book on jurisprudence, the theory and history of law and government.

There is no mention in all this of a book on natural theology. That is the one part of Smith's Glasgow lectures that he was not disposed to develop for publication. There are, however, a few brief references to theology in the *Moral Sentiments*. Why so, if he regarded ethics as independent of theology? It is because theology is not independent of ethics, so that a discussion of ethics might be thought incomplete if nothing were said about its effect on theology.

One of Smith's references even uses theology against those theologians who think religion is essential for ethics.

[2] *Correspondence of Adam Smith*, letter 248. Cf. Ross, *The Life of Adam Smith*, 405.
[3] *Correspondence*, letter 137 to David Hume.

Religion affords such strong motives to the practice of virtue . . . that many have been led to suppose, that religious principles were the sole laudable motives of action. We ought neither, they said, to reward from gratitude, nor punish from resentment. . . . All affections for particular objects, ought to be extinguished in our breast. . . . The sole principle and motive of our conduct in the performance of all those different duties, ought to be a sense that God has commanded us to perform them. I shall not at present take time to examine this opinion particularly; I shall only observe, that we should not have expected to have found it entertained by any sect, who professed themselves of a religion in which, as it is the first precept to love the Lord our God with all our heart . . . so it is the second to love our neighbour as we love ourselves; and we love ourselves surely for our own sakes, and not merely because we are commanded to do so. (*TMS* III. 6. 1)

Of the remaining references to theology, two are important for understanding Smith's own position: one was modified in the sixth edition, the other appeared only in that edition. The first comes at the end of a chapter (part II, section ii, chapter 3) on the 'utility' of a 'constitution of Nature' described in the preceding chapter, namely our sense of justice, remorse, and merit. The discussion in chapter 3 is mainly about the justice of punishment, and the word 'utility' in the title is significant, for much of the discussion is an implicit criticism of what Smith took to be Hume's roughly utilitarian theory of justice. Smith does not name Hume: it was not customary in his time to name explicitly a living author whom you were criticizing, if his book did not bear his name.[4] Smith writes of 'the account commonly given' of the justification of punishment, and in his lectures on jurisprudence he speaks of 'Grotius and other writers' as having held utilitarian theories of punishment. But in this chapter

---

[4] After writing this generalization I recalled that Thomas Reid, Smith's successor at Glasgow, frequently names Hume when criticizing him. But having looked again at Reid's works I find that his practice in fact confirms my generalization in an unusual way. Hume died in 1776. Reid's first book, *Inquiry into the Human Mind*, published in 1764, criticizes Hume not by name but by the description 'the author of the *Treatise of Human Nature*'. His later books, *Essays on the Intellectual Powers of Man* (1785) and *Essays on the Active Powers of Man* (1788), refer quite simply to 'Mr Hume'.

of the *Moral Sentiments* he seems to have especially in mind Hume's view that utility pleases through sympathy.

Smith allows that thought and debate about justice are at times backed up by an appeal to social utility, but he insists that this cannot be the primary notion. 'All men, even the most stupid and unthinking, abhor fraud, perfidy, and injustice, and delight to see them punished. But few men have reflected upon the necessity of justice to the existence of society' (*TMS* ii. ii. 3. 9).

A sophisticated utilitarian would not be disturbed by this argument, for he could say that the common, unthinking reaction is engendered by an automatic acceptance of prevalent social mores. But Smith follows on with a more perceptive argument, which one does not often find in philosophical discussion of justice. It is that thought about justice tends to be focused upon the individual rather than society at large. The sophisticated utilitarian cannot dismiss that argument so easily.

Smith then seeks to reinforce his case by reference to theology. While some crimes are punished with a view to utility, he says, the most heinous kind evoke condemnation for their intrinsic character. If a murderer were to escape punishment, the impartial spectator 'would call upon God' to avenge the crime in the next world. The first edition continues as follows.

For . . . we are so far from imagining that injustice ought to be punished in this life, merely on account of the order of society, which cannot otherwise be maintained, that Nature teaches us to hope, and religion authorises us to expect, that it will be punished, even in a life to come. Our sense of its ill desert pursues it . . . even beyond the grave, though the example of its punishment there cannot serve to deter the rest of mankind, who see it not, who know it not, from being guilty of the like practices here. . . .

That the Deity loves virtue and hates vice . . . not for their own sakes, but for the effects which they tend to produce . . . is not the doctrine of nature, but of an artificial, though ingenious, refinement of philosophy. . . . If we consult our natural sentiments, we are apt to fear, lest before the holiness of God, vice should appear to be more worthy of punishment than the weakness and imperfection of human virtue can ever seem to be of reward. . . . The doctrines of revelation coincide . . . with those original anticipations of nature; and, as they teach us how little we can depend upon the imperfection of our own virtue, so they show us, at the same time, that the most powerful intercession has been made, and that the most dreadful atonement has been paid for our manifold transgressions and iniquities.[5]

The third edition introduced some minor revisions: 'religion authorises' was replaced by the less dogmatic phrase 'religion, we suppose, authorises'; 'not the doctrine of nature . . . refinement of philosophy' became 'not the doctrine of untaught nature but of an artificial refinement of reason and philosophy'; 'we are apt to fear' became 'we are even apt to fear'.

In the sixth edition, however, revision was more drastic. The final paragraph of the first-edition version was deleted and replaced by a single sentence added to the preceding paragraph: 'In every religion, and in every superstition that the world has ever beheld, accordingly, there has been a Tartarus as well as an Elysium; a place provided for the punishment of the wicked, as well as one for the reward of the just.'

The text of the first edition, in its reference to atonement as part of revealed doctrine, implies acceptance of specific Christian belief as well as of natural religion. One of the minor revisions in the third edition ('religion, we suppose, authorises') indicates a little less confidence in revealed doctrine. The sixth edition seems to have abandoned it altogether: the words of this version could have been written by the sceptic Hume.

A similar sign of reservation on Christian doctrine is evident in the second substantial reference to theology. This comes at the end of the second chapter of part III. Smith added a lengthy passage in the second edition in order to reply to Sir Gilbert Elliot's criticism of Smith's view of conscience, as I have recounted in Chapter 5. The added passage was retained, with a few trifling amendments,

---

[5] *TMS*, 1st edn., II. ii. 3 (pp. 202–6). See the Glasgow Edition, II. ii. 3. 12 (pp. 91–2).

in the third, fourth, and fifth editions; but in the sixth edition it was substantially revised and followed by further reflections upon conscience and the hope of divine justice in a life to come. Smith writes with such eloquence about this article of faith that it must represent his own view; but he ends up with an indignant protest against a declaration of Bishop Massillon that one day in the life of a monk is more worthy of heaven than many years of military hardship. Smith quotes Massillon in an English translation that is probably his own; it departs from the French original in three details, two of which seem significant.

First, Massillon writes twice of 'le Seigneur' followed soon afterwards by 'Jésus-Christ'; Smith's translation in both places is 'the Lord' followed by 'Him', avoiding the name of Jesus Christ. Secondly, Massillon says that ten years of military service are more wearing than 'une vie entière de pénitence'; Smith expands the latter phrase to 'a whole life of repentance and mortification'. Massillon does use the word *mortifier* earlier but not in the relevant sentence here. Smith's final paragraph fastens upon his own version.

To compare, in this manner, the futile mortifications of a monastery, to the ennobling hardships and hazards of war; to suppose that one day, or one hour, employed in the former should, in the eye of the great Judge of the world, have more merit than a whole life spent honourably in the latter, is surely contrary to all our moral sentiments... Can we wonder that so strange an application of this most respectable doctrine should sometimes have exposed it to contempt and derision?

And he then quotes a derisive couplet of Voltaire on the Christian idea of hell:

> Vous y grillez sage et docte Platon,
> Divin Homère, éloquent Cicéron.

This addition to the sixth edition of the *Moral Sentiments* may be compared with a passage in *The Wealth of Nations*: 'when moral, as well as natural philosophy, came to be taught only as subservient to theology...heaven was to be earned only by penance and mortification, by the austerities and abasement of a monk.'[6]

I have said that the final version of the passage about atonement could have been written by Hume. That is equally true of the criticism of Massillon. Hume wrote in his *Enquiry concerning the Principles of Morals* (1751): 'penance, mortification, and the whole train of monkish virtues...are...everywhere rejected by men of sense.'[7] In fact I think that Smith had Hume very much in mind when he revised the atonement passage. The relevant chapter is a criticism of a utilitarian view of justice and seems to be aimed particularly at Hume. The original version of the *Moral Sentiments* was published in 1759, when Hume was alive and flourishing. *The Wealth of Nations* was published in 1776, shortly before Hume's death. The thoroughly revised version of the *Moral Sentiments* was written in 1789, barely a year before Smith's own death. I think that when Smith came to write the revised version, he felt that a declaration of Christian doctrine now would be not only dishonest but altogether inappropriate to the context of criticizing his friend Hume; and so he cut it out and substituted a sentiment similar to the one I have quoted from *The Wealth of Nations*. It is, I have written elsewhere, a libation to Hume's ghost.

The history of this passage gave rise to a theological encounter wittily related in John Rae's *Life of Adam Smith*.[8] William Magee, Archbishop of Dublin, published in 1801 a collection of his sermons on the Christian doctrine of atonement. In a second edition of 1809 Magee added some 'illustrations and explanatory dissertations', one of which quoted Adam Smith's mention of the doctrine as it appeared in the original version of the *Moral Sentiments*. Magee took pleasure in the endorsement of Christian teaching by this great philosopher,

---

6 Adam Smith, *An Inquiry into the Nature and Causes of the Wealth of Nations.* ed. R. H. Campbell, A. S. Skinner, and W. B. Todd (Oxford: Clarendon Press, 1976), v. i. f. 30.

7 Hume, *Enquiry concerning the Principles of Morals*, IX. i.

8 Rae, *Life of Adam Smith*, 428–9.

one, moreover, who was 'the familiar friend' of the sceptic David Hume. Magee ended his comment by saying that the views regarded by Smith as 'the natural suggestions of reason' were 'the scoff of sciolists and witlings'. Whereupon the sciolists and witlings took equal pleasure in pointing out that Adam Smith withdrew the passage in the final edition of the *Moral Sentiments*. Magee responded in the next edition of his own book, acknowledging the change, of which he had been ignorant before, and adding that Smith's revision only goes to show how dangerous it is, 'even to the most enlightened', to be in 'familiar contact with infidelity'.

Magee may not have been off the mark in suggesting that Smith's change of heart was due to 'the infection of David Hume's society'. Rae disputes this, both because he thinks there was no change of heart and because Smith's friendship with Hume was very close in 1759, when the *Moral Sentiments* first appeared, while Hume had been long dead when Smith revised the book for the sixth edition of 1790. Rae also notes that the passage about the execution of Jean Calas, added in the sixth edition, includes a statement that religion alone can comfort people like Calas with the hope of justice being eventually done in 'another world'. And so Rae concludes that Smith 'died as he lived, in the full faith of those doctrines of natural religion which he had publicly taught'.

There is indeed no reason to think that Smith ceased to accept the doctrines of natural religion, but that was not the issue for Magee. The words that Smith had originally written clearly implied an acceptance of the specifically Christian doctrine that the death of Jesus Christ atoned for the sins of all mankind, while the revised text of the sixth edition simply speaks of 'religion' generally and finds in 'every religion and every superstition' a notion of divinely ordained reward and punishment to be dealt out in a life after death.

In a letter of 14 August 1776 to Alexander Wedderburn, Smith wrote: 'Poor David Hume is dying very fast, but with great chearfulness and good humour and with more real resignation to the necessary course of things, than any Whining Christian ever dyed with pretended resignation to the will of God.'[9] Smith probably did not intend the last words to apply to all devout Christians, but still they come a long way from his own early acceptance of Christianity. That does not mean that he followed Hume into scepticism. When he revised the *Moral Sentiments* passage on retributive justice, he retained unaltered the statement that 'Nature teaches us to hope' (though he qualified the following phrase that 'religion authorises us to expect') that justice will be done in a life to come.

In Chapter 1 I wrote of John Dunn's description of Adam Smith as a 'practical atheist'. He applies the term also to Hume and tells us that it means 'someone for whom, if God does exist, at least his existence makes no practical difference to the sane conduct of human life'.[10] Dunn implies that for a genuine theist the existence of God does make a practical difference to conduct. What sort of difference? Presumably it concerns virtuous conduct. A theist believes that virtuous actions have been commanded by God and should be done for that reason. A 'practical atheist', if he resembles Adam Smith, does not think he needs that reason: he does virtuous actions for reasons directly connected with the actions themselves—because they have good consequences or prevent bad ones, because they fulfil a promise or other form of undertaking, because they promote equity, because they respect the interests and rights of other persons. The actual actions performed by the two characters are unlikely to differ. The theist may think he has additional duties concerned with religious practice, but his conduct under the rubric of virtue will be no more and no less than that of the 'practical atheist'. He acts in a different spirit but the content and consequences of his action are no different.

Dunn tells us that he borrows the term 'practical atheist' from David Gauthier, writing of Hobbes. When Dunn calls Hume and Smith practical atheists, he seems to imply that they differ from the common run of people. Gauthier, on the other hand, says that, now

---

[9] *Correspondence of Adam Smith*, letter 163.
[10] Dunn, 'From applied theology to social analysis', 119.

at least, pretty well everyone is a practical atheist: 'Although Hobbes is no atheist, he is what we may call a practical atheist—as indeed we, his successors, all are. God makes no difference to the structure of Hobbes's moral and political system.'[11]

It is worth recalling an anecdote about Hobbes in John Aubrey's *Brief Lives*. Hobbes, says Aubrey, was very charitable. On one occasion, seeing 'with eyes of pity and compassion' an old and infirm beggar, Hobbes gave him some money. A cleric, who happened to stand by, asked: 'Would you have done this if it had not been Christ's command?' Hobbes said he would, and when asked why, replied: 'Because I was in pain to consider the miserable condition of the old man; and now my alms, giving him some relief, doth also ease me.' The cleric assumes that Hobbes's motive cannot have been purely 'pity and compassion': there must have been self-interest behind it, the expectation of heavenly reward for obeying divine command. Hobbes's reply, that his motive was to relieve his own pain as much as the pain of the old man, goes along with the cleric's assumption of self-interest, perhaps because the cleric could think only in those terms, or perhaps because of Hobbes's own egoistic theory of motivation.

Does John Dunn make the same assumption as Aubrey's cleric? Does he think that the practical reason for accepting theism must be the self-interested motive of wanting to go to heaven, and that people who have no care for this are therefore practical atheists? If so, Hume and Adam Smith do not fit the picture, because both of them rejected a purely egoistic theory of human motivation.

Hume in his own day was often called an atheist, referring to his belief, not this conduct. He was not an atheist and is reported to have said to the Baron d'Holbach that he did not believe there were any atheists (only to be told that he was in the company of fifteen atheists at that very time). Hume was a sceptic. A sceptic on religion is more positive than an agnostic: he thinks it is probable, but not certain,

11 David Gauthier, 'Why Ought One Obey God? Reflections on Hobbes and Locke', *Canadian Journal of Philosophy*, 7 (1977), 425–62, at 435.

that traditional theology is untrue. In Hume's *Dialogues concerning Natural Religion*, Philo, the character who represents Hume's own views, allows that there is some force in the argument from design but not enough to support the traditional view of God as the source of morality.

Adam Smith was not a sceptic: although he abandoned Christianity, he remained a theist. John Dunn quotes a passage from the *Moral Sentiments* in order to show that Smith was a theist in 1759. As I said in Chapter 1, Dunn is mistaken in attributing this passage (deploring the idea of a fatherless world) to 1759; it was in fact written for the sixth edition of 1790. There are other new passages in the sixth edition that confirm Smith's acceptance of theism.

Religion alone . . . can tell them [people unjustly treated], that it is of little importance what man may think of their conduct, while the all-seeing Judge of the world approves of it. (*TMS* III. 2. 12)

In such cases, the only effectual consolation of humbled and afflicted man lies in an appeal to a still higher tribunal, to that of the all-seeing Judge of the world . . . That there is a world to come, where exact justice will be done to every man . . . is a doctrine . . . that the virtuous man who has the misfortune to doubt of it, cannot possibly avoid wishing most earnestly and anxiously to believe it. It could never have been exposed to the derision of the scoffer, had not the distribution of rewards and punishments, which some of its most zealous assertors have taught us was to be made in that world to come, been too frequently in direct opposition to all our moral sentiments. (*TMS* III. 2. 33)

It is clear from the final words of this quotation, as also from the quotation criticizing Massillon, that Smith's theism in his later years is fashioned by his ethics: a theology is unacceptable if it fails to accord with 'all our moral sentiments'. He is disturbed by theology of that character and is keen to refute it. His refutation consists in showing up the discordance with moral judgement, the bedrock of his outlook on life.

12

Jurisprudence

As one would expect, there is no reference to the impartial spectator in *The Wealth of Nations*. The plural term 'impartial spectators' does occur towards the end of the work, where Smith reflects that distant colonies have little concern about political dispute at the centre of an empire: their distance 'renders them more indifferent and impartial spectators of the conduct' of the contending parties.[1] The words 'impartial spectators' in this passage carry their ordinary sense and have no connection with Smith's special concept of the impartial spectator.

This is not true, however, of Smith's use of the term in his lectures on jurisprudence. There, as in the *Moral Sentiments*, Smith speaks of the impartial (or the indifferent) spectator as providing the criterion of right action. We have a detailed student report of the jurisprudence lectures as given in the academic session 1762–3, and we also have a more summary report, dated 1766, probably of the lectures as given in the session 1763–4. There are some differences between the two, notably in the order of treatment of the various topics, and also, to a limited extent, in the actual subject matter. So far as the impartial spectator is concerned, there is a verbal difference in the adjective used ('impartial' sometimes replaced by 'indifferent') but no difference of substance. The occasional misspellings in my quotations follow the printed version of the two reports, Adam Smith, *Lectures on Jurisprudence* (Oxford: Clarendon Press, 1978), faithfully reproducing what is in the manuscripts.

---

[1] Smith, *Wealth of Nations*, v. iii. 90.

In the report of lectures of 1762–3, which we know to be actual student notes, there are four places in which Smith refers to the view of an impartial spectator as the criterion of moral judgement. He does not use in all four contexts the precise expression 'the [or 'an'] impartial spectator'; more often he speaks simply of 'the spectator'. But it is plain that he does have in mind his special concept of the impartial spectator.

Two of the four uses of the impartial spectator criterion come in Smith's discussion of the rights of property. He lists five sources or grounds of a property right: occupation, tradition, accession, prescription (or *usucapio*), and succession. These are all technical terms of legal usage. Occupation means the first instance of taking possession of something that was not previously the private property of anyone. Tradition is handing over, transferring, ownership to another person, most commonly by sale. Accession is the emergence in a property of an additional entity in the natural course of events: the most obvious example is the birth of young and the development of milk in a female animal; a less obvious example is the growth of crops on a piece of land that has been acquired as property. Prescription is exclusive usage over a long period of time. Succession is the accepted method of transferring ownership on the death of a proprietor.

Adam Smith introduces the judgement of the impartial spectator for two of these five grounds of property right, namely occupation and prescription. Why does he pick out these two? I think it is because, in both of them, one can sensibly ask why the circumstances give rise to a right while nevertheless seeing that the proposition has general agreement. One can intelligibly ask why should taking hold of something in the wild, or having had long usage of a thing or a piece of land, confer a right? There is no logical necessity for such a connection, but it is commonly found and seems intuitively reasonable.

The other three types of case are different. Tradition and accession are so plainly sensible that hardly anyone would dream of asking for a justification. If John Doe chooses to hand over to Richard

Roe a thing that he owns, who could doubt or query that Richard is now the owner? And, if John's cow gives birth to a calf, who could reasonably doubt that John owns the calf as well as the cow? Conceivably one might argue that the owner of the cow's mate, if other than John, could claim part-ownership of the calf; and Smith is careful enough to mention a genuine exceptional case of this character, while also spelling out the reasons for the general rule.

It is to be observed that the young of all animalls is supposed to be an accession to the mother rather than the father. The actions of conceiving, bearing, bringing forth, and suckling appear to produce a much stronger connection betwixt the young and the mother than the transitory act of begetting does with the fathers. . . . There is no exception to this but in the swans, where it is the rule that part of the young goes to the proprietor of the male and part goes to that of the female; the reason given is that as the male cohabits only with one female he could be of no benefit to his owner unless he got part of the young he had produced.[2]

Unlike tradition and accession, succession is anything but plain. Testamentary succession, that is, inheritance in accordance with the instructions of a will, is clear enough, but this is a relatively late development. Non-testamentary succession has taken different forms in different societies, for example, on primogeniture and more notably on the inclusion or exclusion of females among inheritors; so it cannot be said that any one form would receive general agreement as being morally right.

There is, therefore, no scope for the determining judgement of the impartial spectator in any of these three sources of a right of property. Tradition and accession are too obvious to need any judgement, while succession has been so varied that it cannot be subjected to a firm criterion.

Smith himself does not spell out the argument I have suggested for confining the impartial spectator to the remaining two types of property right, occupation and prescription. He does, however,

[2] Smith, *Lectures on Jurisprudence*, LJ(A) i. §§64–5.

see them as similar in depending on the reasonable expectation of the right-holder. Because the expectation is reasonable, it wins the sympathy of spectators.

The first thing to be attended to is how occupation, that is, the bare possession of a subject, comes to give us an exclusive right to the subject so acquired.—How is it that a man by pulling an apple should be imagined to have a right to that apple and a power of excluding all others from it—and that an injury should be conceived to be done when such a subject is taken [from] the possessor. From the system I have already explain'd . . . we may conceive an injury was done when an impartial spectator would be of opinion he was injured, would join with him in his concern and go along with him when he defended the subject in his possession against any violent attack. . . . The cause of this sympathy or concurrence betwixt the spectator and the possessor is, that he enters into his thoughts and concurrs in his opinion that he may form a reasonable expectation of using the fruit . . . in what manner he pleases. . . . The reasonable expectation therefore which the first possessor furnishes is the ground on which the right of property is acquired by occupation. You may ask indeed, as this apple is as fit for your use as it is for mine, what title have I to detain it from you. You may go to the forest (says one to me) and pull another. You may go as well as I, replied I. And besides it is more reasonable that you should, as I have gone already and bestowed my time and pains in procuring the fruit.[3]

[The] right of prescription is in fact derived from the same principles as that of occupation. For in the same manner as the spectator can enter into the expectations of the 1st occupant that he will have the use of the thing occupied, and think he is injured by those who would wrest it from him; in the same manner, the right of prescription is derived from the opinion of the spectator that the possessor of a long standing has a just expectation that he may use what has been thus possessed.[4]

When illustrating the right of occupation with the example of plucking an apple, Smith distinguishes the breach of a right from an unfair trespass upon common practices of possession, which an impartial spectator would think wrong but not so heinous as to

---

[3] Smith, *Lectures on Jurisprudence*, LJ(A) i. §§35–7.   [4] Ibid., LJ(A) i. §77.

be the breach of a right. He imagines one man seizing an apple that another man was about to pluck: 'an impartial spectator would conceive this was a very great breach of good manners and civility but would not suppose it an incroachment on property.' Smith adds that one can go even further. If the apple-picker plucks his apple and happens to drop it, and then the other man seizes it, 'this would be still more uncivil and a very heinous affront, bordering very near on a breach of the right of property', but still not an actual breach. There would be an actual breach of a right if the first man was holding the apple in his hand and the second man tried to snatch it. In those circumstances 'the bystander would immediately agree that . . . property was incroached on'.[5]

The example of gathering apples brings to mind John Locke's discussion of the rights of property in his *Second Treatise: Of Civil Government*. It is possible, perhaps likely, that Adam Smith too had it in mind. Locke founds the initial right of acquiring property in 'mixing one's labour' with things in a natural state; and he illustrates this with the examples of picking up acorns or gathering apples from trees. If Smith was thinking of Locke's account, he was probably offering his own view as an alternative, or a supplementary, explanation.

Why would he do that? Because the expression 'mixing one's labour' is a metaphor, not plainly enlightening. Locke says that 'every man has a property in his own person' and therefore 'the labour of his body, and the work of his hands, we may say, are properly his'. When he removes something from its natural state, 'he hath mixed his labour with, and joyned to it something that is his own, and thereby makes it his property'.[6] The argument comes to this: a man's body, including his hands, is his own, belongs to him and not to anyone else; and therefore anything that the work of his hands has changed belongs to him. But the meaning of 'belongs' is ambiguous. It is rather odd to say that a man's body belongs to him, but less odd to say that his hands belong to him, are his own, meaning really that his hands are part of him. If one now says that

---

[5] Ibid., LJ(A) i. §42.   [6] John Locke, *The Second Treatise of Government* §27.

the work of his hands belongs to him, one certainly does not mean that the work of his hands is part of him like the hands themselves.

Is Adam Smith's account an improvement upon Locke's? The sympathy of an impartial spectator is not the ground of the apple-picker's right of ownership; it confirms the apple picker's judgement but is not the reason why that judgement is sound. Smith is well aware of this: in the passage quoted above about occupation, he distinguishes 'the cause' of the spectator's sympathy from that 'sympathy or concurrence' itself. He says that the ground of the first possessor's right is his reasonable expectation; and the expectation is reasonable because he has spent 'time and pains' on acquiring the fruit. So in the end Smith's explanation is a labour theory, but superior to Locke's because it does not introduce the confusing metaphor of 'mixing' one's labour and treating the work of one's hands as an extension of the hands. As often, Smith sticks to common sense and is persuasive for that reason.

So much for the role of the impartial spectator on the topic of property rights. The other two contexts in which the impartial spectator appears (in the 1762–3 lectures on jurisprudence) are contract and delinquency. In discussing contract Smith distinguishes between expressing an intention and making a promise.

Now it appears evident that a bare declaration of will to do such or such a thing can not produce an obligation. It means no more than that it is the present design of the person . . . to do so and so . . . The only thing that can make an obligation in this manner is an open and plain declaration that he desires the person to whom he makes the declaration to have a dependance on what he promises. The words in which we commonly make such a declaration are I promise to do so and so, you may depend upon it. The expectation and dependance of the promittee that he shall obtain what was promised is hear altogether reasonable, and such as an impartial spectator would readily go along with, whereas in the former case [i.e. the mere expression of an intention] the spectator could not go along with him if he formed any great expectation.[7]

[7] Smith, *Lectures on Jurisprudence*, LJ(A) ii. §§42–3.

Delinquency, that is, the culpable causing of damage to others, gives rise to a right of those others to be 'repaid'. Smith takes this repayment to include punishment when the damage was wilful, and here too he brings in the impartial spectator to determine the appropriate measure of punishment. The specific question to be asked is, 'How far would the impartial spectator sympathize with the resentment of the injured party in retaliating the harm done to him?' As in the *Moral Sentiments*, Smith rejects a purely utilitarian account of punishment, pointing to the difference in public attitude towards punishments inflicted for genuine crimes and punishments based on utility. He notes that the death penalty for murder has public approval, but statutes (enacted in the reigns of Henry VI and Charles II) that prescribed the death penalty for the export of wool were simply unworkable.

This exportation was no crime at all, in naturall equity, and was very far from deserving so high a punishment in the eyes of the people; they therefore found that while this was the punishment they could get neither jury nor informers. No one would consent to the punishment of a thing in itself so innocent by so high a penalty. They were therefore obliged to lessen the punishment to a confiscation of goods and vessel.[8]

Smith then goes on to cite an even more telling example, which he describes also in the *Moral Sentiments* and in the earlier manuscript of a lecture on justice that I have mentioned in Chapter 1.

In the same manner the military laws punish a centinell who falls asleep upon guard with death. This is intirely founded on the consideration of the publick good; and tho we may perhaps approve of the sacrificing one person for the safety of a few, yet such a punishment when it is inflicted affects us in a very different manner from that of a cruel murtherer or other atrocious criminall.[9]

This was a real-life example that may have been related to Smith as a recollection of his father, who served for a time as Clerk of the Court

8 Ibid., LJ(A) ii. §§91–2.   9 Ibid., LJ(A) ii. §92.

Martial in Scotland.[10] The version in the *Moral Sentiments* conveys
more vividly the depth of Smith's feelings about the case.

Upon some occasions, indeed, we both punish and approve of punishment,
merely from a view to the general interest of society, which, we imagine,
cannot otherwise be secured.... A centinel, for example, who falls asleep
upon his watch, suffers death by the laws of war, because such carelessness
might endanger the whole army.... Yet this punishment, how necessary
soever, always appears to be excessively severe. The natural atrocity of
the crime seems to be so little, and the punishment so great, that it is
with great difficulty that our heart can reconcile itself to it.... A man
of humanity must... exert his whole firmness and resolution, before he
can bring himself... to go along with it.... It is not, however, in this
manner, that he looks upon the just punishment of an ungrateful murderer
or parricide.... The very different sentiments with which the spectator
views those different punishments, is a proof that his approbation of the
one is far from being founded upon the same principles with that of the
other. He looks upon the centinel as an unfortunate victim, who, indeed,
must, and ought to be, devoted to the safety of numbers, but whom
still, in his heart, he would be glad to save; and he is only sorry, that
the interest of the many should oppose it. But if the murderer should
escape from punishment, it would excite his highest indignation, and
he would call upon God to avenge, in another world, that crime which
the injustice of mankind had neglected to chastise upon earth. (*TMS* II.
ii. 3. 11)

That completes the account of the role of the impartial spectator in
the jurisprudence lectures of 1762–3. The report of 1766 does not
add anything; it is altogether a briefer discussion and mentions the
impartial spectator in connection with occupation, prescription, and
delinquency. Its account of contract does not include any mention
of the spectator.

Occupation seems to be well founded when the spectator can go along with
my possession of the object, and approve me when I defend my possession

---

[10] W. R. Scott, *Adam Smith as Student and Professor* (Glasgow: Jackson, Son & Co.,
1937), 129; Ross, *The Life of Adam Smith*, 4–6.

by force. If I have gathered some wild fruit it will appear reasonable to the spectator that I should dispose of it as I please.[11]

There are four things requisite to form a right by prescription. 1st, bona fides, for if a person be sensible that his right to a thing is bad it is no injury to deprive him of it, and the indifferent spectator can easily go along with the depriving him of the possession. 2^d, iustus titulus . . . some reasonable foundation that the person has to think a thing his own, such as a charter of some kind. If he claims a right without any such tittle no impartial spectator can enter into his sentiments.[12]

Injury naturaly excites the resentment of the spectator, and the punishment of the offender is reasonable as far as the indifferent spectator can go along with it. This is the natural measure of punishment.[13]

In Chapter 5 I have argued that Smith's concept of the impartial spectator was developed as a theory about conscience, the capacity to make judgements on one's own actions, past or contemplated. Much of my evidence was taken from the new part VI of the sixth edition of the *Moral Sentiments*, written in 1789, but a fair amount of significant evidence related to the second edition, published at the end of 1760 (and imprinted 1761). In the present chapter I have described the references to the impartial spectator in Smith's lectures on jurisprudence as delivered in the academic sessions 1762N3 and (probably) 1763N4. None of these references are confined to judgements about oneself. Some of them are concerned with property rights, others with the justification of punishment, and one with the rights acquired by contract. So it seems that in his actual lectures in his last two sessions at Glasgow Smith did not associate the notion of the impartial spectator with judgements about oneself. Does this cast doubt on my view that Smith was beginning to develop the concept in 1760 as a theory of conscience, of judgements about oneself?

I think not. There was no reason why he should *confine* his use of the expression to moral judgements about oneself when he was

[11] Smith, *Lectures on Jurisprudence*, LJ(B) §150.   [12] Ibid., LJ(B) §154.
[13] Ibid., LJ(B) §181.

discussing other parts of his course of Moral Philosophy. Judgements about oneself are matters for ethics, not jurisprudence; so it was perfectly natural for Smith, in his lectures on law, as on economics, to speak of impartial spectators in a literal sense. It remains true that the printed version of his theory of ethics in the *Moral Sentiments* gave a special sense to 'the impartial spectator' as an interpretation of conscience—which is not to say that his usage of the term in the *Moral Sentiments* is confined to that special sense.

13

Ethics and Economics

'The Adam Smith problem' concerned the relation between ethics and economics in Smith's thought. The point of controversy was whether there is an inconsistency between the *Moral Sentiments* and *The Wealth of Nations* on the psychology of human action. The *Moral Sentiments*, it was alleged, treats altruistic sympathy as the motive of virtuous action, while *The Wealth of Nations* regards self-interest as the motive of all human action.

Such a crude interpretation of Smith's thought could arise only from a failure to read his writings with care. The scholars who took up the alleged problem were, in general, interested in Smith's economics and not well versed in philosophy. They had little understanding of Smith's theory of moral judgement, the context in which sympathy is given prominence. They were also rather careless in supposing that remarks about self-interest were intended to cover all action.

Take the colourful example that comes early in *The Wealth of Nations*: 'It is not from the benevolence of the butcher, the brewer, or the baker, that we expect our dinner, but from their regard to their own interest.'[1] This is, of course, meant to have a fairly wide application but not so wide as to take in all human actions. Smith goes on to say: 'Nobody but a beggar chuses to depend chiefly upon the benevolence of his fellow-citizens. Even a beggar does not depend upon it entirely.' Nobody but a beggar depends *chiefly* on benevolence and even the beggar does not depend on it *entirely*. That implies that we do all depend on benevolence to

---

[1] Smith, *Wealth of Nations*, I. ii. 2.

some extent. The main point of the passage, to be sure, is that we would be foolish to count on benevolence for most of what we want: we should in general expect people to think of their self-interest. Nevertheless the passage does not warrant an assumption that all action is self-interested.

As for sympathy, it is prominent in Smith's ethics, not as a motive of action, but as a constituent of moral judgement, and that is irrelevant to any question of consistency in Smith's views on the motivation of conduct. This particular feature, however, is not as simple as the one about self-interest. Sympathy is *prominent* in Smith's ethics as a prime element of moral judgement, but there are passages in the *Moral Sentiments* where sympathy appears as a motive. It could hardly be otherwise, since that is a fact of life. We are, from time to time, prompted to do helpful actions for other people from sympathy with their plight or needs; and anyone writing about ethics is likely to mention such actions as a typical form of moral conduct. If such a writer chooses, as Adam Smith does, to give sympathy a central role in a different aspect of the subject, namely moral judgement, he will nevertheless find it difficult to avoid mentioning sympathy in its familiar role as a frequent element of moral action.

You might say, therefore, that Smith himself bears some responsibility for the misunderstanding that formed the Adam Smith problem, especially since two instances of his mention of sympathy as a motive occur in the context of political economy. The invisible hand passage of the *Moral Sentiments* is followed by reflections on the motivation of public improvements.

When a patriot exerts himself for the improvement of any part of the public police, his conduct does not always arise from pure sympathy with the happiness of those who are to reap the benefit of it. It is not commonly from a fellow-feeling with carriers and waggoners that a public-spirited man encourages the mending of high roads. When the legislature establishes premiums and other encouragements to advance the linen or woollen manufactures, its conduct seldom proceeds from pure sympathy with the wearer of cheap or fine cloth, and much less from that with the manufacturer or merchant. (*TMS* IV. 1. 11)

That passage, coming just after the invisible hand, would be likely to catch the attention of readers mainly interested in Smith's economics, and they might well have supposed that his use of the term 'sympathy' here is typical of his normal use. Still, they would have taken a different view if they had read the whole of the book with any care. They could have seen from the very first chapters that Smith thinks of sympathy as the key to understanding moral judgement and that he explicitly distinguishes his use of the term from that of a synonym for pity or compassion. 'Pity and compassion are words appropriated to signify our fellow-feeling with the sorrow of others. Sympathy, though its meaning was, perhaps, originally the same, may now, however, without much impropriety, be made use of to denote our fellow-feeling with any passion whatever' (*TMS* I. i. 1.5).

It may be as well to recall briefly the main players in the saga of the Adam Smith problem. It began in Germany. Bruno Hildebrand, writing in 1848 a general work on the progress of economics, described *The Wealth of Nations* as 'materialist', meaning that it was based on a psychology of egoism. Then Karl Knies, likewise writing a history of economics in 1853, brought in the *Moral Sentiments* too, suggesting that Adam Smith took different views of human psychology in his two books and that the change was due to his residence in Paris for a few months of 1766, where he met a group of French economists known as the Physiocrats. An English historian, Henry Thomas Buckle, in his *History of Civilisation in England*, has a chapter on Scottish thought in the eighteenth century, evidently counting that as part of 'civilisation in England'. He certainly cannot have read Smith's books with care. He takes them to cover 'the two divisions of a single subject', the sympathetic and the selfish aspects of human nature, 'a primary and exhaustive division of our motives to action'.[2]

[2] H. T. Buckle, *History of Civilisation in England* (1857–61), ii. 432–3.

After that absurd picture of Smith's work, one is tempted to mitigate criticism of the arch proponent of the Adam Smith problem, Witold von Skarżyński, who was much influenced by Buckle when he wrote in 1878 a book specifically on Adam Smith as moral philosopher and economist. However, he was himself a ridiculously harsh critic of Smith, maintaining that Smith lacked originality, having learned his moral philosophy from Hutcheson and Hume, and his economics from the French Physiocrats. He also sardonically derided reports (recorded by Dugald Stewart in 1793) that Smith's lectures at Glasgow included the gist of *The Wealth of Nations*. On the matter of inconsistency, Skarżyński took Buckle to have shown that Smith's two books give different accounts of human motivation and so he concluded that Smith changed his mind as a result of discussion with the Physiocrats.

The Adam Smith problem was effectively dissolved with the publication, by Edwin Cannan in 1896, of the 1766 report of Smith's lectures at Glasgow on jurisprudence, including his thought on economics. It should not have been necessary to wait for this, since, as I have said, the *Moral Sentiments* highlights the role of sympathy in judgement, not in motivation.

Traces of the alleged problem have remained even after Cannan's publication. The most notable occurs in a renowned article (mentioned in Chapter 1) by Jacob Viner.[3] It is renowned for showing that Smith's advocacy of laissez-faire is qualified by some serious limitations; but its distinction is marred by a preliminary contrast between *The Wealth of Nations* and the *Moral Sentiments*. According to Viner, the ethics book reflects a youthful idealism that is inconsistent with the mature, realistic thought of the great work on economics.

Viner supported his view of the *Moral Sentiments* by quoting at length five passages from the work. The first of them, describing the widely held idea of a benevolent God, was written for the sixth edition of 1790 and so is later than *The Wealth of Nations*. The second

---

[3] Viner, 'Adam Smith and Laissez Faire'.

says that 'self-preservation, and the propagation of the species, are the great ends which Nature seems to have proposed in the formation of all animals' (*TMS* II. i. 5. 10). There is nothing idealistic about that: any pre-Darwinian scientist would have regarded it as a realistic inference from observed fact. The third and fifth passages, which go together in the *Moral Sentiments* but are separated by Viner, are equally realistic. They say that the non-moral virtues of industry, prudence, and circumspection are generally successful and reap the reward of wealth and honour, while our natural feelings would prefer to see reward going to moral virtue rather than the economic virtue of industry, which can be shown by bad men as well as good. Only the fourth of Viner's five quotations is idealistic: it is the invisible-hand passage with its claim that in 'the real happiness of human life' the poor are 'in no respect inferior' to the rich (*TMS* IV. 1. 10).

Thus Jacob Viner in 1927. By 1968 he had seen the light, though in a glass, darkly. I say 'darkly' because the later article,[4] while giving a sounder account of the *Moral Sentiments*, replaces the charge of inconsistency with the idea that Smith worked with systems or models and moved in his two books from one 'partial model' to another. That sounds like an alternative version of Buckle's position. Viner would have done better to confine himself to the economics, on which he was enlightening.

Practically all scholars with specialized knowledge of Smith's work would now agree that the Adam Smith problem was misconceived. I have come upon only one dissident, Leonidas Montes, who wrote a long article published in 2003.[5] It is mainly an admirably detailed account of the history of the Adam Smith problem, but it also seeks to defend the problem's validity. The precise nature of the defence is rather obscure, but the main point seems to be that Smith thinks of sympathy not only as an element of moral judgement but also

---

[4] Jacob Viner, 'Adam Smith', *International Encyclopedia of the Social Sciences* (New York, 1968).

[5] Leonidas Montes, 'Das Adam Smith Problem', *Journal of the History of Economic Thought*, 25 (2003), 63–90.

as a motive to action. I have acknowledged this in what I have written above (and in my Past Masters book *Adam Smith*, with which Montes is familiar) and have pointed out that Smith makes clear his essential view of sympathy in the first chapters of the *Moral Sentiments*.

A different perspective on the relation between Adam Smith's two books is given by Vivienne Brown and Samuel Fleischacker, whom I mentioned in Chapter 1 as having taken note of the difference between the sixth and the earlier editions of the *Moral Sentiments*.

Vivienne Brown makes the point that the new part VI, added to the sixth edition, has a number of references to legislators and statesmen, whereas the earlier editions have just a few passing mentions of these words, with minimal significance.[6] She concludes that Smith's concern in these references to legislators and statesmen is purely ethical and is unconnected with 'the science of a legislator' described in *The Wealth of Nations* (book IV, introduction) as a master discipline, of which political economy is a branch.

Her own concern is not with any change in Smith's view of ethics but with an alleged difference of style between his two books: she claims that the *Moral Sentiments* is 'dialogic' and *The Wealth of Nations* 'monologic'. She takes these terms from Mikhail Bakhtin, who uses them to describe a distinction between the serious novel (and some moral philosophy), on the one hand, and scientific writing, on the other. According to Bakhtin, dialogic discourse enlists a variety of 'voices' expressing different social or cultural outlooks, while monologic discourse confines itself to a single dominating 'voice' that leaves no room for alternatives.

Some earlier scholars have expressed views about a supposed difference of style between Smith's two books. J. R. McCulloch said that *The Wealth of Nations* was diffuse in style, because it had been dictated to an amanuensis, while the *Moral Sentiments* was not diffuse, because it had not been dictated. But John Rae, reporting

6 Brown, *Adam Smith's Discourse*, 134–40.

this, took the opposite view himself, that 'there is probably more diffuse writing' in the *Moral Sentiments*, while the *Wealth* 'is for the most part packed tightly enough'.[7] I would not venture to join in this debate about style. As for non-stylistic differences between Smith's two books, I would not want to question Vivienne Brown's account of *The Wealth of Nations*, since she is an economist and I am not. But I do question her conclusion about legislators and statesmen in the *Moral Sentiments*. The main point is that the expression 'legislators and statesmen' is prominent in the sixth edition and inconsequential in earlier editions. Vivienne Brown argues, fairly enough, that it should, therefore, not be linked to *The Wealth of Nations*. But it does not follow that Smith's use of the phrase is purely ethical—if 'ethical' is distinguished, as it should be, from social and political. The phrase 'legislators and statesmen' may be divorced from economics, but not from thought about politics. Indeed, the fact that Smith introduced the phrase more prominently in the sixth edition of the *Moral Sentiments* suggests a connection with his wider knowledge and experience at that late stage of his life, including the deep thought and wide inquiry that had gone into writing *The Wealth of Nations*.

A more serious defect in Vivienne Brown's account of Smith's moral philosophy concerns the concept of justice. She says that both the *Lectures on Jurisprudence* and the *Moral Sentiments* 'separate moral judgment from the virtue of justice'.[8] She thinks Smith maintains that 'only beneficence and self-command constitute truly moral virtues while justice and prudence are ... lower-order virtues'; more precisely, that 'the spectatorial account of moral judgment in TMS strictly pertains only to the higher-order virtues, the truly "moral virtues" of beneficence and self-command, and that the lower-order virtues of justice and prudence, which concern the economic domain and the market-place, lie outside the domain of moral discourse proper.'[9] It is true that Smith regarded prudence

---

[7] John Rae, *Life of Adam Smith* (London: Macmillan, 1895; repr. New York, Kelley, 1965), 260–1.

[8] Brown, *Adam Smith's Discourse*, 112.   [9] Ibid. 5, 26.

as a lower-order virtue, but it is a curious error to say the same of justice.

Vivienne Brown connects this interpretation with her distinction between dialogic and monologic discourse, apparently taking Smith's account of justice to_be monologic because he says the rules of justice are precise, and so she divorces justice from morality proper. It is possible that she was also influenced by the fact that, in the new part VI added to the sixth edition, Smith writes at length about beneficence and self-command, with a lesser discussion of prudence and only a brief reference to justice. I have given my own explanation of this in Chapter 8. If Vivienne Brown had paid more attention to part II, she would have seen that Smith there highlights justice and beneficence together, clearly as the two primary moral virtues, and then concentrates on justice.

Samuel Fleischacker's consideration of the different editions of the *Moral Sentiments* is more far-reaching.[10] His book is primarily concerned with the philosophical significance of *The Wealth of Nations*, but he takes account of the whole of Smith's writings, including the *Lectures on Jurisprudence* and even the surviving fragment of a lecture on justice that I mentioned in Chapter 1. He concludes from his meticulous survey that Smith's experience of life led him to become more radical as he grew older.

What is distinctive about Adam Smith's ethics, according to Fleischacker? In a word, egalitarianism. He writes of Smith's advocacy of 'equality of treatment' in *The Wealth of Nations*, though that is not evidence for equality of ability or talents supposedly affirmed in the *Moral Sentiments*. Smith's ethical thought is conveyed primarily in the *Moral Sentiments*, and you would not associate Smith with egalitarianism if you were to read the *Moral Sentiments* alone. There is no clear suggestion of egalitarianism in that book, unless one were to count as egalitarian a snatch of romantic fantasy in the invisible-hand passage. It says that, even in the material inequalities of society as we know it, the poor are not inferior to the rich: 'In ease

---

10 Fleischacker, *On Adam Smith's Wealth of Nations*.

of body and peace of mind, all the different ranks of life are nearly upon a level, and the beggar, who suns himself by the side of the highway, possesses that security which kings are fighting for' (*TMS* IV. 1. 10). But even this is not strict egalitarianism: the different ranks are 'nearly', not quite, upon a level.

In *The Wealth of Nations* the most striking of relevant passages is a well-known comparison between a philosopher and a porter: 'The difference between the most dissimilar characters, between a philosopher and a common street porter, for example, seems to arise not so much from nature, as from habit, custom, and education.'[11] Even here, however, Smith does not espouse egalitarianism proper. He undoubtedly thinks that social distinctions do not reflect natural, innate, differences of potential talent, but he does not deny the existence of natural differences. In his remarks about the philosopher and the porter, he goes on to say that in their infancy the two were 'perhaps very much alike', so that parents and playfellows could not perceive 'any remarkable difference'. After that early age there is a change: 'The difference of talents comes then to be taken notice of, and widens by degrees.'

Fleischacker does not overlook, but tends to belittle, the qualified character of Smith's egalitarianism. He describes his own view as attributing a 'strong moral egalitarianism' to Smith and says that 'Smith appears to have been committed to a remarkably strong version of the claim that people are essentially equal in abilities'.[12] I doubt this: the passage about the philosopher and the porter is the strongest expression of Smith's view on the topic, and it does not say that the natural abilities of the two are essentially equal; it says that in their infancy they were '*perhaps* very much *alike*', so that others could not perceive 'any *remarkable* difference'.

I must add, however, that an earlier version of this passage in Smith's lectures on jurisprudence in 1762–3 does go further. 'No two persons can be more different in their genius as a philosopher

---

[11] Smith, *Wealth of Nations*, I. ii. 4.
[12] Fleischacker, *On Adam Smith's Wealth of Nations*, 208, 76.

and a porter, but there does not seem to have been <?any> originall difference betwixt them. For the 5 or 6 first years of their lives there was hardly any apparent difference; their companions looked upon them as persons of pretty much the same stamp.'[13] Yet even this is not unequivocal: the first sentence appears to assert initial equality, but the second sentence qualifies it with '*hardly any* apparent difference' and '*pretty much* the same stamp'. What is quite clear is a definite qualification in the later version given in *The Wealth of Nations*, so it cannot be true that Smith was 'committed to a remarkably strong' form of egalitarianism. Still, although Fleischacker exaggerates, he does make a valid case for seeing Adam Smith as a radical.

This does not necessarily mean that he was always a radical. A vital part of Fleischacker's view is that Smith progressed to a greater radicalism as he grew older, an unusual form of development, since most people of a radical tendency are apt to moderate it as they advance in years. Fleischacker thinks that the inegalitarian passages of the *Moral Sentiments* belong to the first edition and the egalitarian to the sixth edition.

I cannot follow him in this claim. Smith's comparison between the philosopher and the porter is less radical in *The Wealth of Nations* (1776) than in the lectures of 1762–3. As for the *Moral Sentiments*, the major passages that were added to the sixth edition are chapter 2 of part III and the whole of part VI. There is a theological statement in III. 2 that might be regarded as egalitarian. 'The all-wise Author of Nature has . . . made man . . . the immediate judge of mankind; and has, in this respect, as in many others, created him after his own image' (*TMS* III. 2. 31). One could say this implies that God created *all* men after his own image and so implies an equality of worth among all men. But the sentence, although added in the sixth edition, replaces an addition to the second edition that says the same thing: 'the author of nature has made man the immediate judge of mankind, and has, in this respect, as in many others, created him after his own image.' What is more, a slightly later passage in the

---

[13] Smith, *Lectures on Jurisprudence*, LJ(A), vi. §47.

sixth edition version clearly implies that it is not true that all men are equal, at any rate in moral worth.

> That there is a world to come, where exact justice will be done to every man, where every man will be ranked with those who, in the moral and intellectual qualities, are really his equals; where the owner of... humble talents and virtues... will be placed upon a level, and sometimes above those who, in this world, had enjoyed the highest reputation... is a doctrine... that the virtuous man who has the misfortune to doubt of it, cannot possibly avoid wishing... to believe it. (*TMS* III. 2. 33)

Smith then goes on to deride the view of Massillon that the life of a monk is superior to that of a soldier. He does not imply that the two lives are equal; he clearly thinks that the life of the soldier is superior.

A perusal of the new part VI confirms, I think, that Smith did not accept egalitarianism. In the first section he writes of credit and rank 'among our equals', implying that there are people who are not our equals; and similarly he says that the prudent man 'is willing to place himself rather below than above his equals' (*TMS* VI. i. 3–4; VI. i. 10). In the third section he says that many persons who are unable to read, write, or do simple arithmetic have been led by pride to 'set themselves upon a level with their equals in age and situation' (*TMS* VI. iii. 49). He clearly believes that equality in age and situation can coexist with inequality in human worth. (He distinguishes these people from idiots, who are conscious of their 'great inferiority', and who are not relevant to Smith's view of the generality of mankind.) A little later he says that the proud man 'is tormented with indignation at the unjust superiority, as he thinks it, of other people' (*TMS* VI. iii. 51). The words 'as he thinks it' imply that Smith himself thinks otherwise: the fancied superiority of others may be well grounded.

However, I must concede that additional evidence from Professor Fleischacker gives me pause. In correspondence with me he has cited two places in part II of the *Moral Sentiments* where egalitarianism can be found. The first is II. ii. 2. 1, where Smith says that, although every man is liable to rate his own happiness as more important to him 'than that of all the world besides', he knows that to others 'he is but one of a multitude in no respect better than any other in it'. The second passage is in II. ii. 3. 10, where Smith says that our concern for redress to an injured individual 'is no more than the general fellow-feeling which we have with every man merely because he is our fellow-creature'. These statements do indeed imply that there is a basic equality in our evaluation of and concern for other people. It is at any rate clear that Fleischacker has elicited, from the two books taken together, that Adam Smith's thought rested on a radical outlook, a fact that I think has not been appreciated by earlier commentators.

14

Smith's Enduring Contribution

The work of a philosopher of the past may be studied from a historical or from a philosophical perspective. The historical treatment considers the work in relation to the time at which it was written: how it was affected by the events of that time and perhaps of earlier times, including earlier philosophical works that may have influenced the author; and also how this work itself has or may have influenced later works of philosophy. The philosophical treatment considers the work in a spirit of critical debate, just as it might consider a philosophical book of its own time, evaluating the author's arguments and replying to them if found wanting. My approach to Adam Smith's *Moral Sentiments* in this book has mainly taken the philosophical perspective, though I have occasionally dipped into history, as when I surveyed spectator theory in Chapter 4, and when I asked, in Chapter 10, whether Smith could have seen performances of the works of drama that he cites. In this final chapter, continuing the philosophical treatment, I consider whether Smith's moral philosophy contains any enduring contribution to the subject, a contribution that philosophers of the present day should take seriously for their own deliberations. I think that there is such a contribution in Smith's concept of the impartial spectator.

That is the chief legacy of the work but it is not the only one. Smith continually refers to the role of spectators in other aspects of moral thought—real spectators, not the ideal impartial spectator, though real spectators too are free from partiality and that is the point for Smith of bringing them into his discussion. So virtually the whole book is affected by the viewpoint of spectators; it constitutes the typical character of Smith's moral philosophy. One topic that is especially worthy of note is his account of fairness that I have described in Chapter 9.

The notion of fairness is easily grasped; children pick it up very soon and are ready to complain of treatment that is 'not fair'. Yet the concept is not easily analysed and Smith's reference to spectators is a help towards bringing out its particular nuance. He compares decency of behaviour towards others with competition in a race and says that, if one of the runners tries to gain an advantage by jostling another, he is immediately condemned by spectators as a violator of 'fair play'. They are ready to allow for the dominance of self-interest as a motive, but it applies equally to everyone. They sympathize with the resentment of the second runner, who to them is just as good as the jostler.

I turn now to Smith's distinctive development of the impartial spectator. In Chapter 6 I said that Smith's theory of moral judgement on one's own actions was too complicated to be acceptable; but I also said that the criticism arises from his account of approval and that his concept of the impartial spectator seems persuasive when taken with an unanalysed notion of approval. That persuasive element is what I see as his enduring contribution. It is a genetic theory of conscience, a speculative hypothesis of the origin of conscience. Its essence lies in the social experience of being a spectator of the conduct of other persons and of knowing that others are spectators of one's own conduct. This experience leads us to imagine, not what others think of our deeds (we do not need imagination to learn of that), but what they would think if they had all the relevant information that each of us has from our own awareness of motive and intention. If they had that, they would be well-informed and impartial spectators—informed to a degree that they cannot be in fact, and impartial because they are not practically involved and so not liable to be swayed by self-interest, as the agent himself is. But if the agent is liable to be swayed by self-interest, how can *he* reach an impartial judgement? He can do so because the imagination can free itself from the ties of practical desires.

It is an ingenious theory. Can we test its truth? How do we test the truth of any genetic theory of mental phenomena? It is hard to say, and it is uncertain whether there can be reliable testing of such a theory. The study of psychology, originally conceived as the science of mind, has been diverted to the science of behaviour because mental phenomena are not susceptible to the methods of inquiry employed in the physical and biological sciences. Behaviour, like physical objects, animals, and plants, is publicly observable, and the reported observations of any one person or group of persons can be verified or falsified by the observations of other persons. This is not true of mental phenomena. We do have good reason, from communication with each other, to think that, generally speaking, we have common mental experiences; and we can understand, again from communication, that there are aberrations, as in colour blindness or tone deafness. These aberrations show up the subjectivity, and hence uncertainty, of mental experience. Still, that does not rule out the acquisition of fairly reliable knowledge of what is generally true of mental states. We can judge its reliability by the apparent coherence of our own mental states with the reported mental states of other people and by the absence of incoherence with observable fact. That is not a foolproof test of truth, but it does provide support for credibility.

Adam Smith's theory of conscience seems to me to pass this test. I do not know of any alternative theory that is more persuasive. I have written in Chapter 6 of its superiority to Freud's account of conscience on the ground that Freud's view is too narrow in relation to observable facts (that is, if it is interpreted as a general theory of conscience and not simply as a pragmatic hypothesis for the medical treatment of neurosis).

I had thought it likely that Max Scheler's book *The Nature of Sympathy* would contain an alternative view of conscience based on sympathy, but found that in fact it repudiates the idea. As for other German moral philosophers, Nicolai Hartmann's monumental *Ethics* has a fair amount to say about the role of conscience but nothing about its genesis, and Leonard Nelson's *System of Ethics* is equally silent on this topic. So are the French thinkers of whom I have any knowledge, and likewise the American. So far as British moral philosophers are concerned, Bishop Butler gives conscience a crucial role in his account of moral judgement, but he does not have any theory of its genesis: he simply regards conscience as part of the divine endowment of human nature.

It would be comforting to be able to support Smith's speculative theory with some publicly observable evidence. Can this perhaps be done in considering any instances of a human being who has had no contact with other human beings? There is a record of one person who apparently had been out of contact with other human beings from early childhood until found in his early teens. He is known as Peter the 'Wild Boy' and was discovered in 1725 in a wood near Hamelin, living in trees like a squirrel.

He was visited by the eighteenth-century Scottish judge and philosopher Lord Monboddo (James Burnett), whose interest was to seek support for his evolutionary theory that early man was little, if at all, more intelligent than the ape. Monboddo writes briefly of Peter in his book on *The Origin and Progress of Language*, but says nothing about any relevance for ethics.[1] There is more information about Peter in *The Book of Wonderful Characters* by Henry Wilson and James Caulfield.[2] When Peter was found, he was estimated to be about 13 years old. He was presented to King George I, who was in Hanover at the time. Peter could not speak and never learned to say anything much other than the name Peter given to him and the name of his patron King George, though he did learn to understand what was said to him. Monboddo visited him when he was about 70, living in a farmhouse in Berkhamstead on a pension provided by the King. With his virtual incapacity for language, Peter could hardly be said to have acquired a conscience, though he was evidently a gentle sort of being. However, this information about Peter the Wild

[1] James Burnett, Lord Monboddo, *The Origin and Progress of Language* (1773), I. i. 14; p. 186. Monboddo simply mentions Peter as 'a mute savage that was caught in the woods of Hanover'.

[2] Henry Wilson and James Caulfield, *The Book of Wonderful Characters* (1869), 133–40.

Boy simply indicates that the development of conscience depends on living in society. It is evidence against the view of Bishop Butler that conscience is a God-given endowment, but it is not evidence supportive of a specific theory of social origin.

Reflection on British moral philosophers prompts a different question: what is the philosophical relevance of a genetic theory of conscience? Suppose we grant that Adam Smith makes a good case for his genetic theory: how does that bring enlightenment for philosophy? I said in Chapter 6 that offering a genetic theory of conscience is not a task that would be undertaken by present-day philosophers; but I also added that 'fortunately' the division of labour had not been carried that far in Adam Smith's day. Why 'fortunately'? Is it a task that *should* be performed by philosophers? Well, I think they can learn from it, whether or not they themselves tackle it.

Present-day philosophers would of course agree that the results of scientific study can be relevant to their concerns: when they analyse thought or language, they must take account of facts, and facts include established conclusions of scientific inquiry. Adam Smith's genetic theory of conscience does not fall within that category: it depends on facts of experience in the form of introspection, but these are not scientific facts, since they are not publicly observable so as to be open to refutation. Still, they are familiar facts accessible to everyone. The novelty in Smith's theory lies in his use of imagination to draw from familiar facts a striking hypothesis that seems entirely credible although nobody else has thought of it. He resembles a good scientist, except that the scientist, more often than not, relies on newly discovered as well as familiar facts.

A more significant difference is that the scientist not only draws his theory from facts; he also turns to further facts to test the theory. It used to be commonly said that the testing was a matter of aiming to confirm a hypothesis; confirm, not prove, because strict proof, in inductive reasoning, would require observation of every single instance of the facts covered by the hypothesis. Karl Popper put forward an alternative view that the logic of scientific discovery is deductive, not inductive, and that it consists in the attempt to refute a hypothesis by finding an instance that does not conform to the hypothesis and so (deductively) proving its falsity as a universal law. The hypothesis takes the form 'All S is P'; the negative instance X shows that 'X is an S but is not P'; and hence it follows that the hypothesis 'All S is P' is false. According to Popper, a scientific hypothesis that has withstood such refutation has been 'corroborated' and may be accepted as established for practical purposes.

It is hard to see how such testing can be adequately applied to Adam Smith's theory of conscience. I have declared Smith's theory to be superior to Freud's because it takes in a wider range of relevant evidence: it explains both positive and negative judgements of conscience and attributes the genesis of conscience to a variety of causal agencies (parents, teachers, schoolfellows), while Freud concentrates on the negative features of disapproval and fear of punishment, and on the causal agency of parents alone. The evidence to which I have alluded consists of observable facts. So far, so good. But how can one try to refute Smith's theory? Peter the Wild Boy would be a relevant example if he had shown signs of having a conscience despite having no experience of being affected by spectators; but it seems inconceivable that anyone could have a conscience without some grasp of language use. The origin of language is a mystery, and that must be true of the origin of conscience too. All we can say is that Adam Smith's theory is a plausible suggestion. It does strike one as having the ring of truth, and in the absence of refutation it seems to be well founded.

Hard-headed sceptics, however, may object that a purely hypothetical explanation of genesis cannot be treated as a foundation for truth. Truth is a value-laden concept and cannot just be bundled into a basket of facts. To say that a statement is true implies that we ought to believe it, and 'An "ought", if it is to be derived at all, can only be derived from another "ought" '.[3] The classic source of this

---

[3] H. A. Prichard, 'Does Moral Philosophy Rest on a Mistake?', *Mind*, 21 (1912); repr. in Prichard, *Moral Obligation* (Oxford: Clarendon Press, 1949) and in Prichard, *Moral Writings*, ed. Jim MacAdam (Oxford: Clarendon Press, 2002).

thought is an argument given by Hume in his refutation of ethical rationalism. It has now become something of a shibboleth that an 'ought' cannot be derived from an 'is'. Let us see just what Hume wrote.

In every system of morality, which I have hitherto met with, I have always remark'd, that the author proceeds for some time in the ordinary way of reasoning ... when of a sudden I am surpriz'd to find, that instead of the usual copulations of propositions, *is*, and *is not*, I meet with no proposition that is not connected with an *ought*, or an *ought not*. This change is imperceptible; but is, however, of the last consequence. For as this *ought*, or *ought not*, expresses some new relation or affirmation, 'tis necessary that it shou'd be observ'd and explain'd; and ... that a reason should be given, for what seems altogether inconceivable, how this new relation can be a deduction from others, that are entirely different from it.[4]

Hume writes of a *deduction*, and it is, of course, true that the conclusion of a deductive inference cannot validly contain a term that was not included in the premises. Prichard was making the same point in saying that an 'ought' can only be 'derived' from another 'ought'; 'derived' meant deduced. But one can speak of being derived in a non-logical sense, and indeed Hume uses the term in this way. His argument about 'is' and 'ought' comes at the end of a section entitled 'Moral Distinctions not deriv'd from Reason' and is followed by another section entitled 'Moral distinctions deriv'd from a moral sense'. The title of the latter section obviously cannot mean that moral distinctions are *deduced* from a moral sense, and the earlier arguments in the former section ('Moral Distinctions not deriv'd from Reason') include some non-logical considerations.

If we take the notion of derivation in a broad sense that is not confined to deduction, I think it is not true to say that an 'ought' cannot be derived from an 'is', or (to put the same point in another way) that an imperative cannot be derived from an indicative. I call the Bible to witness.

---

[4] Hume, *A Treatise of Human Nature*, III. i. 1. last para; ed. Selby-Bigge, 469.

The Israelites are commanded in several places to love the stranger, and the commandment is grounded on the fact that they themselves had been strangers in Egypt. Leviticus 19: 34 says 'thou shalt love him [the stranger] as thyself; for ye were strangers in the land of Egypt'. Deuteronomy 10: 19 repeats the same thought: 'Love ye therefore the stranger: for ye were strangers in the land of Egypt.' The Israelites are apparently told that they *ought* to love the stranger *because* they *had been* strangers themselves. Are we to accuse the writers of the Bible of committing a logical error in grounding a commandment on a fact, in deriving an 'ought' from an 'is'?

No, there is no logical error: the grounding is psychological, not logical. A fuller statement of the underlying thought in this commandment is given in Exodus 23: 9: 'thou shalt not oppress a stranger: for ye know the heart of a stranger, seeing ye were strangers in the land of Egypt.' This comes near to the thought of Adam Smith. The normative statement is grounded on fellow-feeling, sympathy: having been strangers, you know what it feels like to be an outsider, to be deprived of the warm affection that is given to friends and relations. The inference is not claiming that past experience of being a stranger is the reason why we ought to be kind to strangers; it is saying that our past experience makes us capable of understanding the feelings of strangers, enabling us to sympathize, to feel as they do. It assumes that the sympathy aroused by memory of our own experience will generally, as a matter of course, but not inevitably, prompt us to be kind to strangers. The assumption is perfectly reasonable, depending on familiar evidence of everyday life. A cynic who claims to reply on logic could respond to the biblical commandment: 'Even if I was once a stranger, I am not a stranger now and I feel no obligation to help strangers.' He may have logic on his side but he would be thought a monster, not a rational human being.

What, then, endures from Adam Smith's moral philosophy? It connects moral judgement with social relationship in a novel way, explaining its origin by reference to the reaction of spectators. The most interesting feature of the account is its application to conscience, judgement about one's own behaviour: it explains this as a complex reaction to the feelings of approval and disapproval by disinterested spectators. That gives conscience a social origin and a social function.

Smith's theory of conscience is a hypothesis that conscience is derived from social relationship, and therefore that the moral use of the word 'ought' is derived from situations described in purely positive terms. This is psychological derivation, not logical, but that does not bar it from being of philosophical interest. If we wish to understand conscience and moral judgement, we do well to take account of psychology and sociology as well as logic; and that purpose is exceptionally well served by Adam Smith in *The Theory of Moral Sentiments*.

Bibliography

Works used or cited in the course of this book

AUBREY, JOHN, *Brief Lives* (1898).

BALGUY, JOHN, *The Foundation of Moral Goodness*, pt. I (1728); pt. II (1729).

—— *A Collection of Tracts Moral and Theological* (1734); includes reprint of both parts of *The Foundation of Moral Goodness*.

BROWN, VIVIENNE, *Adam Smith's Discourse* (London and New York: Routledge, 1994).

BUCKLE, H. T., *History of Civilisation in England* (1857–61).

BUTLER, JOSEPH, *Fifteen Sermons preached at the Rolls Chapel* (1726).

—— 'Dissertation of the Nature of Virtue', appended to *The Analogy of Religion* (1736).

CAMPBELL, T. D., *Adam Smith's Science of Morals* (London: George Allen & Unwin, 1971).

CLARKE, SAMUEL, *A Discourse concerning the Unchangeable Obligations of Natural Religion* (1706).

DAICHES, DAVID, *Edinburgh* (London: Hamish Hamilton, 1978).

DARWALL, STEPHEN, 'Sympathetic Liberalism: Recent Work on Adam Smith', *Philosophy and Public Affairs*, 28 (1999).

DUNN, JOHN, 'From applied theology to social analysis: the break between John Locke and the Scottish Enlightenment', in Istvan Hont and Michael Ignatieff (eds.), *Wealth and Virtue* (Cambridge: Cambridge University Press, 1983).

FIRTH, RODERICK, 'Ethical Absolutism and the Ideal Observer', *Philosophy and Phenomenological Research*, 12 (1952).

FLEISCHACKER, SAMUEL, *On Adam Smith's Wealth of Nations* (Princeton: Princeton University Press, 2004).

FREUD, SIGMUND, *Das Ich und das Es* (1923); English translation by Joan Riviere, *The Ego and the Id* (London: Hogarth Press, 1927).

—— *Das Unbehagen in der Kultur* (1929–30); English translation by Joan Riviere, *Civilization and its Discontents* (London: Hogarth Press, 1963).

GAUTHIER, DAVID, 'Why Ought One Obey God? Reflections on Hobbes and Locke', *Canadian Journal of Philosophy*, 7 (1977).

GRISWOLD, CHARLES L., Jr., *Adam Smith and the Virtues of Enlightenment* (Cambridge: Cambridge University Press, 1999).

HAAKONSSEN, KNUD, *The Science of a Legislator* (Cambridge: Cambridge University Press, 1981).

HARMAN, GILBERT, *Moral Agent and Impartial Spectator* (University of Kansas, 1986).

HILDEBRAND, BRUNO, *Die Nationalökonomie der Gegenwart und Zukunft* (1848).

HOBBES, THOMAS, *Human Nature* (1650).

——*Leviathan* (1651).

HUME, DAVID, *A Treatise of Human Nature*, bks. I–II (1739); bk. III (1740); ed. L. A. Selby-Bigge (Oxford: Clarendon Press, 1896; revised by P. H. Nidditch, 1978); ed. David Fate Norton and Mary J. Norton (Oxford: Oxford University Press, 2000).

——*An Enquiry concerning the Principles of Morals* (1751); included in *Enquiries concerning the Human Understanding and concerning the Principles of Morals*, ed. L. A. Selby-Bigge (Oxford: Clarendon Press, 1893; revised by P. H. Nidditch, 1975); ed. Tom L. Beauchamp (Oxford: Clarendon Press, 1998).

——*Letters of David Hume*, ed. J. Y. T. Greig (Oxford: Clarendon Press, 1932).

HUTCHESON, FRANCIS, *An Inquiry into the original of our Ideas of Beauty and Virtue* (rev. 4th edn., 1738); the second of the two treatises is entitled *An Inquiry concerning Moral Good and Evil*.

——*An Essay on the Nature and Conduct of the Passions and Affections. With Illustrations on the Moral Sense* (1728; 3rd edn., 1742).

——*A System of Moral Philosophy* (1755).

——*Francis Hutcheson: Philosophical Writings*, ed. R. S. Downie (London: Dent, 1994).

KAMES, HENRY HOME, LORD, *Essays on the Principles of Morality and Natural Religion* (1751).

KNIES, KARL G. A., *Die Politische Oekonomie vom Standpunkte der geschichtlichen Methode* (1853).

LOCKE, JOHN, *The Second Treatise*, in *Two Treatises of Government* (1690; 3rd edn., 1698), ed. Peter Laslett (Cambridge: Cambridge University Press, 1960; 2nd edn. with amendments, 1970).

McCULLOCH, J. R., reported in Rae, *Life of Adam Smith*.

MACFIE, A. L., *The Individual in Society: Papers on Adam Smith* (London: Allen & Unwin, 1967).

MAGEE, WILLIAM, *Discourses on the Scriptural Doctrines of Atonement and Sacrifice* (2nd edn., 1809), Dissertations 22 and 69.

MARSHALL, DAVID, *The Figure of Theater* (New York: Columbia University Press, 1986).

MASSILLON, JEAN-BAPTISTE, *Discours . . . [au] régiment de Catinat* (included in *Le Petit Carême*, 1718).

MONBODDO, JAMES BURNETT, LORD, *The Origin and Progress of Language* (1773).

MONTES, LEONIDAS, 'Das Adam Smith Problem', *Journal of the History of Economic Thought*, 25 (2003).

NUSSBAUM, MARTHA, *Love's Knowledge* (New York and Oxford: Oxford University Press, 1990).

—— *Upheavals of Thought* (Cambridge: Cambridge University Press, 2001).

PRICE, RICHARD, *A Review of the Principal Questions and Difficulties in Morals* (1758; 3rd edn., 1787); ed. D. D. Raphael (Oxford: Clarendon Press, 1948; corrected reprint, 1974).

PRICHARD, H. A., 'Does Moral Philosophy Rest on a Mistake?', *Mind*, 21 (1912); reprinted in Prichard, *Moral Obligation* (Oxford: Clarendon Press, 1949), and in Prichard, *Moral Writings*, ed. Jim MacAdam (Oxford: Clarendon Press, 2002).

RAE, JOHN, *Life of Adam Smith* (London: Macmillan, 1895; repr. New York: Kelley, 1965).

RAPHAEL, D. D. (ed.), *British Moralists 1650–1800* (Oxford: Clarendon Press, 1969; repr. Indianapolis: Hackett, 1991).

—— 'Adam Smith and "the infection of David Hume's society" ', *Journal of the History of Ideas*, 30 (1969), repr. (revised and corrected) as appendix II of the Glasgow Edition of Adam Smith, *The Theory of Moral Sentiments*.

RAWLS, JOHN, *A Theory of Justice* (Cambridge, Mass.: Harvard University Press, 1971; Oxford: Clarendon Press, 1972; rev. edn., 1999).

REID, THOMAS, *An Inquiry into the Human mind, on the Principles of Common Sense* (1764).

—— *Essays on the Intellectual Powers of Man* (1785).

_____ *Essays on the Active Powers of Man* (1788); reprinted in vol. iii of *Essays on the Powers of the Human Mind* (Edinburgh: Bell & Bradfute; London: Longman, etc., 1808).

Ross, Ian Simpson, *The Life of Adam Smith* (Oxford: Clarendon Press, 1995).

Rothschild, Emma, *Economic Sentiments: Adam Smith, Condorcet, and the Enlightenment* (Cambridge, Mass., and London: Harvard University Press, 2001).

Schneider, H. W. (ed.), *Adam Smith's Moral and Political Philosophy* (New York: Hafner, 1948).

Scott, W. R., *Adam Smith as Student and Professor* (Glasgow: Jackson, Son & Co., 1937).

_____ *Adam Smith: An Oration* (Glasgow: Glasgow University Publications, No. 48, 1938).

Selby-Bigge, L. A. (ed.), *British Moralists* (Oxford: Clarendon Press, 1897).

Shaftesbury, Anthony Ashley Cooper, 3rd Earl of, *An Inquiry concerning Virtue, or Merit* (unauthorized 1st edn., 1699; corrected 2nd edn., 1714).

_____ *The Moralists: a philosophical rhapsody* (1709).

_____ *Characteristics of Men, Manners, Opinions, and Times* (1711) (includes reprints of the two earlier works, the *Inquiry* in a corrected version); ed. L. E. Klein (Cambridge: Cambridge University Press, 1999).

Skarżyński, Witold von, *Adam Smith als Moralphilosoph und Schoepfer der Nationaloekonomie* (1878).

Smith, Adam, *The Theory of Moral Sentiments* (1759; 6th edn., 1790); the Glasgow Edition, ed. D. D. Raphael and A. L. Macfie (Oxford: Clarendon Press, 1976; corrected reprint, 1991).

_____ *An Inquiry into the Nature and Causes of the Wealth of Nations* (1776; 3rd edn., 1784); the Glasgow Edition, ed. R. H. Campbell, A. S. Skinner, and W. B. Todd (Oxford: Clarendon Press, 1976).

_____ *Lectures on Justice, Police, Revenue and Arms*, ed. Edwin Cannan (Oxford: Clarendon Press, 1896).

_____ *Lectures on Jurisprudence*, ed. R. L. Meek, D. D. Raphael, and P. G. Stein (Oxford: Clarendon Press, 1978).

_____ *The Correspondence of Adam Smith*, ed. E. C. Mossner and I. S. Ross (Oxford: Clarendon Press, 1977; 2nd edn., corrected and enlarged, 1987).

VINER, JACOB, 'Adam Smith and Laissez Faire', *Journal of Political Economy*, 35 (1927); reprinted in Viner, *The Long View and the Short* (Glencoe, Ill., 1958).

—— 'Adam Smith', *International Encyclopedia of the Social Sciences* (New York, 1968).

VIVENZA, GLORIA, *Adam Smith e la cultura classica* (Pisa: Il pensiero economico moderno, 1984); English version, revised and enlarged, *Adam Smith and the Classics* (Oxford: Oxford University Press, 2001).

VOLTAIRE (FRANÇOIS MARIE AROUET), *La Pucelle d'Orléans* (1755).

WILSON, HENRY, and CAULFIELD, JAMES, *The Book of Wonderful Characters* (1869).

WOLLASTON, WILLIAM, *The Religion of Nature delineated* (1724).

Index

Adam Smith problem 1, 115–20
aesthetics 19, 28, 59–60, 68, 82, 85, 87, 92–3
Alembert, Jean Le Rond d' 78
approval 14, 16–21, 25, 52, 60, 72
Aristotle 70–1, 73
atheist 103
  practical 2, 102–3
Aubrey, John 103
authority 58

Bakhtin, Mikhail 120
Balguy, John 83–4
beauty 28, 81–8, 92–3
beneficence 66–8, 74–8, 121–2
benevolence 28–9, 40, 65, 66–7, 70–2, 115–16
  universal 76, 78–9
Black, Joseph 95
Brown, Vivienne 3–4, 120–2
Buccleuch, Henry Scott, 3rd Duke of 39, 63
Buckle, Henry T. 117–19
Burns, Robert 34 n.
Butler, Bishop Joseph 27–8, 49–50, 57–8, 60–1, 130–1
Butler, Samuel 9

Cadell, Thomas 69–70
Calas, Jean 38–9, 101
Campbell, Tom D. 3–4, 44
Cannan, Edwin 118
Caulfield, James 130
Christianity 8, 34, 40, 63, 67, 96, 98–103
Clarke, Samuel 6, 70–1
conscience:
  in Butler 58, 60–1, 131

  in Smith 31, 34–42, 48–52, 67, 98–9, 113–14
  testing theory of 128–9, 132, 134–5
consequences 23–5, 90
contract 110
courage 73

Darwall, Stephen 3–4
delinquency 111
d'Holbach, Baron 103
disinterested 27–8, 30
drama 90–2
Dunn, John 2, 102–4

economics 68, 90, 94, 116–17, 119, 121
egalitarianism 122–6
egoistic 27, 103, 117
Elliot, Sir Gilbert 32, 36–8, 67, 98
empiricists 27, 49–50
Epicurus 71, 73

fairness 74–5, 128
Firth, Roderick 43–4, 47
Fleischacker, Samuel 3–4, 120, 122–6
Freud, Sigmund 48–9, 129, 132

Gauthier, David 102–3
Glasgow University 5, 32, 91
God:
  and conscience 37–8, 44–5
  doctrine on 97, 102–4, 118
  laws of 54, 56, 58, 61, 63–4
Griswold, Charles L. 2–3, 5, 14 n.
Grotius, Hugo 96

Haakonssen, Knud 3–4
Harman, Gilbert 43

Hartmann, Nicolai 129
Hildebrand, Bruno 117
Hobbes, Thomas 9, 48, 81–2, 88, 102–3
humanity 34, 40, 66–7
Hume, David:
  as critic 6–7, 18
  criticized 22, 40, 47, 71, 93, 96–7
  influence of 25–6, 46, 56, 67, 88, 98, 100–4, 118
  thought of 27, 29–31, 33–4, 49, 63, 84–5, 87, 133
Hutcheson, Francis:
  as critic 6
  criticized 22, 40, 50, 57
  influence of 88, 93, 118
  thought of 7, 27–9, 31, 33–4, 49, 70–1, 82–3, 87
Hutton, James 95

imagination 12–16, 21, 38, 40, 50, 128, 131
induction 53–5
intention 22–4, 110
invisible hand 4–5, 90, 116–17, 119, 122

jurisprudence 5–6, 66, 94–5, 118, 123–4
justice:
  commutative 75
  and fairness 74–5
  in Hume 30
  and the individual 97
  lecture on 5, 32–3
  and merit 74–5
  and need 76
  positive and negative 66
  among virtues 67–8, 74–6, 121–2

Kames, Henry Home, Lord 85–8
Knies, Karl 117

laissez-faire 2, 118
La Rochefoucauld, François, Duc de 65
La Rochefoucauld, Louis Alexandre, Duc de 65, 69, 95
law 58, 63
Locke, John 83, 109–10
love, Christian 67

McCulloch, J. R. 120
Macfie, Alec L. 5, 34 n., 67
Magee, Archbishop William 100–1
Mandeville, Bernard 65, 82
Marshall, David 2 n.
Massillon, Bishop Jean Baptiste 73, 99–100, 104, 125
merit 22–6, 31, 63, 66, 68
Monboddo, James Burnett, Lord 130
Montes, Leonidas 119–20
moral judgement:
  in Butler 27–8, 58
  first-person 51
  in Hutcheson 27–8
  logic of 55
  in Shaftesbury 27–8
  in Smith 7, 10–11, 13–20, 22–4
  superiority of 59–60
  theory of 68–9, 128
moral sens, 7, 25, 28–9, 31, 50, 57, 83, 133
moral sentiment 29

nature 54, 56, 62–3, 72, 76, 90
Nelson, Leonard 129
Nussbaum, Martha 43

opinion 19–21

Peter the Wild Boy 130–2
Physiocrats 117–18
Plato 70–1, 73
Popper, Sir Karl R. 131–2
Price, Richard 87–8

Prichard, H. A. 132–3
promise 110
property rights 106–10, 112–13
propriety 13–14, 16–18, 21–5, 65,
    68, 70–2, 92
    dist. virtue 72
prudence 60–1, 65, 66–8, 70–3,
    121–2
    superior and inferior 68, 74
psychology:
    of affection 76–7
    egoistic 27, 117
    of moral judgement 7, 28, 47–50,
        117, 135
    of motivation 115
    as science of behaviour 129
punishment 74–5, 111–12

Rae, John 91, 100–1, 120–1
rationalists 27, 31, 50, 53, 55
Rawls, John 43–8
Reid, Thomas 76, 96n.
religion 56–7, 63, 98, 101,
    103–4
Rothschild, Emma 3–5

sceptic 102–4
Scheler, Max 129
Scott, W. R. 52
self-command 11, 34, 40–1, 66–8,
    79–80, 121–2
self-deceit 54
self-interest 27, 60–1, 65, 73, 75,
    103, 115–16, 128
senses 58–9, 83
Shaftesbury, Anthony Ashley Cooper,
    3rd Earl of 27–8, 71, 81–3, 88
Skarżyński, Witold von 118
sociology 7–8, 47, 50, 68
spectator(s) 9, 15–17, 31, 42, 44–5,
    127
    impartial 11, 30, 32–8, 40–2, 45,
        47, 51–2, 105–7, 114,
        127–8

in Hume 30
in Hutcheson 28–9
in Rawls 45–6
    theory 31
Stewart, Dugald 118
Stoics 4, 34, 40, 67, 71
sympathy:
    in Bible 134
    habitual 76–7
    in Hume 29, 31, 47
    and merit 22, 24–5, 31,
        47
    in moral judgement 9, 12–21,
        116–19
    and motive 21–2, 24, 31, 46,
        115, 120
    in Smith 31, 71

theist 102–4
theologians 50, 53
theology 57, 61, 63, 94–8, 100–1,
    104, 124

utility 46–7, 68, 71, 88, 96–7

Viner, Jacob 2, 4, 118–19
virtue(s):
    amiable and respectable 66
    and beauty 81–9, 92–3
    cardinal 73–80
    character of 10–11, 28, 65–7,
        69–72
    justification of 27–8
    natural and artificial 7, 29–30
    dist. propriety 72
Vivenza, Gloria 3–4
Voltaire 39, 99

Wealth of Nations 1–3, 46, 90,
    94–5, 99–100, 105, 115, 118,
    120–4
Wedderburn, Alexander 101
Wilson, Henry 130
Wollaston, William 6, 71